Western Europe in
Soviet Global Strategy

Western Europe in Soviet Global Strategy

edited by
**Ray S. Cline,
James Arnold Miller,
and Roger E. Kanet**

Westview Press / Boulder and London

Westview Special Studies on the Soviet Union and Eastern Europe

The views expressed in these chapters are those of the authors and not necessarily those of the participating institutions. This report on Western Europe and Soviet global strategy was prepared by the U.S. Global Strategy Council.

Chairman: Dr. Ray S. Cline
President: Dr. Michael A. Daniels
Executive Director: Dr. James Arnold Miller

Project editor: Marjorie W. Cline
Assistant to the project editor: Christopher S. Carver

This Westview softcover edition is printed on acid-free paper and bound in softcovers that carry the highest rating of the National Association of State Textbook Administrators, in consultation with the Association of American Publishers and the Book Manufacturers' Institute.

Copyright © 1987 by Westview Press, Inc.

Published in 1987 in the United States of America by Westview Press, Inc.; Frederick A. Praeger, Publisher; 5500 Central Avenue, Boulder, Colorado 80301

Library of Congress Cataloging-in-Publication Data
Western Europe in Soviet global strategy/edited by Ray S. Cline,
    James Arnold Miller, and Roger E. Kanet.
        p.   cm.—(Westview special studies on the Soviet Union and
    Eastern Europe)
        Includes index.
        ISBN 0-8133-7480-4
        1. Soviet Union—National security.   2. Soviet Union—Military
    relations—Europe.   3. Europe—Military relations—Soviet Union.
    4. Communist strategy.   I. Cline, Ray S.   II. Miller, James A.
    (James Arnold)   III. Kanet, Roger E., 1936–   .   IV. Series.
    UA770.S6617   1987
    355'.0335'47—dc19   87-22474
                                                                                                CIP

Composition for this book was provided by the editors.
This book was produced without formal editing by the publisher.

Printed and bound in the United States of America

∞   The paper used in this publication meets the requirements of the American National Standard for Permanence of Paper for Printed Library Materials Z39.48-1984.

6   5   4   3   2

CONTENTS

PREFACE

Soviet global strategy, long established and well understood by the Kremlin leaders, is to intimidate weak and fearful governments, exploit indigenous difficulties, disrupt social order, and promote communist revolutions. In this volume, European and American scholars describe the USSR's land and sea targets on and surrounding West Europe, where the Soviet Union systematically engages its political, economic, and military instruments of national power to expand its strength.

It is our belief that, taken together, the papers which we have selected for inclusion comprise a useful backdrop for assessing current Soviet interests and activities on the European continent. They develop the basic Soviet doctrine as it is applied to West Germany, the northern and southern flanks of NATO, and the developing nations of the so-called Third World. They recall how the Kremlin leaders trumpet notions of "peace" as Soviet military forces continue their buildup. Whether by calling their policies "detente," "peaceful coexistence," or glasnost, Soviet leaders from Lenin to Gorbachev regularly attempt to lull the people of the Free World into complacency.

The scholars presented papers for this volume under the auspices of the Soviet Global Strategy Project, an undertaking of 1983-1985 by Interaction Systems Incorporated of McLean, Virginia, and the World Strategy Network, now associated with the United States Global Strategy Council of Washington, D.C. The West European aspect of the project included the holding of two conferences: (1) in Rome on May 16-17, 1984, co-sponsored by Rome's Instituto di Studi Europei "Alcide de Gasperi" and (2) in West Germany on January 6-8, 1985, at the Christian-Albrechts-University in Kiel, co-sponsored by the University's Institute of Security Studies.

The planning, research, and presentation of the papers were funded by the Office of Policy Support, Office of the U.S. Secretary of Defense. The papers, however, do not necessarily reflect the policies and positions of the Department of Defense.

The project has been continued as an important activity of the United States Global Strategy Council, a recently organized non-profit research institution dedicated to studying strategic issues as they apply not only to the United States but also to the whole Free World.

It is with great pride that we present, on behalf of all the parties associated with this effort, this volume of the final report of the Soviet Global Strategy Project.

Ray S. Cline
James Arnold Miller
Roger E. Kanet

Chapter 1

INTRODUCTION TO BASIC SOVIET GEOPOLITICS

Ray S. Cline

Political leaders in the USSR from Lenin to Mikhail Gorbachev have articulated and tried to follow -- not always with complete success -- coordinated, coherent, long-range plans to advance Soviet national goals in the world arena. They have uniformly viewed international relations as a scene of irreconcilable zero-sum conflict between their totally government controlled socio-economic system and the pluralist states with economies based on private capitalist enterprise. They explicitly say they seek to expand Soviet influence until such time as all nations are Soviet-style socialist states governed under the principles of Leninist doctrine or at least weak client states dominated by the military and economic power of the Soviet Union.

Soviet leaders have repeatedly explained that they are following a policy of "detente," a term that literally means, in French, a stopping or release of tension. In the United States, however, the meaning has become ambiguous. In 1971 and 1972, detente -- in the language of U.S.-USSR diplomatic relations -- originally meant simply a relaxation of tension which would permit Moscow and Washington to enter into a dialogue or a negotiating process that might reduce confrontations and dangers of war.

As time went on, the Nixon administration claimed such enormous benefits from personal diplomacy in Moscow and Peking that the term came to carry with it a connotation of peace and international harmony favorable to U.S. security and welfare. By 1975, many people in the United States had come to think that detente meant:

o   a guarantee of peace, in the sense of avoidance of all kinds of war;

o   stability in the international relations of governments and in social order;

2

- o   coordination and friendly cooperation between great powers, including the United States and the USSR; and

- o   tolerance of differing social systems, even as different as those in the United States and the USSR.

Unfortunately, this widespread U.S. understanding of detente conflicts with the basic interpretation which the USSR has always had of what it originally quite scrupulously referred to as "peaceful coexistence." From the very beginning, Soviet doctrinal literature, in explaining to the cadres and officialdom as well as to the people of the Soviet Union what peaceful coexistence meant, took a quite different line.

The USSR puts a heavy emphasis on "peace" -- even as the United States does -- but Soviet leaders obviously mean by it only the avoidance of total nuclear war between the United States and the Soviet Union. This meaning was clear during the many years of U.S. weapons superiority. They did not want international issues settled in a contest in which the USSR was the weaker nation.

Soviet leaders have consistently espoused the right to fight a "just war" of "national liberation," that is, to assist a country to shake off external domination, as they would say they were doing in Vietnam. Beyond that, they have made painfully clear, especially for the benefit of their own citizenry, that peaceful coexistence, in addition to avoiding total war, means:

- o   unrelenting class struggle;

- o   worldwide support of the forces of revolution by the ballot if possible and by violence if necessary;

- o   diplomatic moves to bring about political realignments in non-communist areas so as to restrict the parts of the world open to U.S. influence, trade, investment, and procurement of economic raw materials; and

- o   permanent positive antipathy between the communist and capitalist social systems, the latter of which, according to Soviet doctrine, is still supposed to perish in the ultimate and long-heralded "world crisis of capitalism."

Soviet statements for the past seven decades have carefully restricted the meaning of peaceful coexistence to fit this classical Marxist-Leninist theory of social conflict. Lenin stated in 1919 the world view of the generation of Bolshevik rulers who had seized power in 1917:

We are living not merely in a state, but in a system of states and the existence of the Soviet Republic side by side with imperialist states for a long time is unthinkable. One or the other must triumph in the end.[1]

The clearest theoretical pronouncement of the Soviet world view came from Stalin shortly before his death in March 1953:

The disintegration of a single universal world market must be considered the most important economic consequence of the Second World War. . . . This circumstance determined the further aggravation of the general crisis in the world capitalist system. . . . It follows . . . that the sphere of exploitation of world resources by the major capitalist countries (USA, Britain, France) will not expand but contract, that the world market conditions will deteriorate for these countries and that the number of enterprises operating at less than capacity will multiply in these countries. It is this essentially which constitutes the aggravation of the general crisis in the world capitalist system due to disintegration of the world market . . . .[2]

Brezhnev reaffirmed the Soviet adherence to Lenin's conception of the inevitability of the clash between capitalism and communism in his report to the 24th Congress of the Communist Party of the Soviet Union (CPSU), March 30, 1971:

In recognition of its international duty, the CPSU will continue to pursue a line in international affairs which promotes the further activation of the world anti-imperialist struggle and strengthens the combat unity of all its participants. The total triumph of Socialism the world over is inevitable. And for this triumph, for the happiness of the working people, we will fight, unsparing of our strength.[3]

There are many statements by Soviet officials of this central idea. A particularly direct formulation was made December 21, 1972, not long after President Nixon's euphoric summit visit to Moscow, when Brezhnev explained:

The CPSU has always held and still holds that the class struggle between the two systems -- the capitalist and the socialist -- in the economic, political and also, of course, in the ideological spheres will continue. It cannot be otherwise, because the world outlook and class aims of socialism and capitalism are opposed and irreconcilable. But we will strive to shift this historically inevitable struggle onto a path which

4

will not threaten wars, dangerous conflicts, an unrestricted arms race.[4]

Since the mid-1950s, under Khrushchev's leadership, military assistance and economic aid on a massive scale were sent to countries which the USSR hoped could be won away from economic and political relations with the United States or West European "capitalist" powers. While not so generous as Khrushchev, Brezhnev continued to use arms and money to gain influence over peripheral areas and deny them to the West. Particularly in the Mideast, Soviet policy has brought a major change in the patterns of stability in this region and jeopardized the access of the United States, West Europe, and Japan to the oil which is vital to their industries.

The heady impression Moscow gained from watching the removal of a U.S. president and the diffusion of leadership in the United States provided the strategic underpinning of the entire peaceful coexistence or detente policy of the 1970s. The Soviet Union insists that the evolving world situation -- in what Soviet ideologues call the "correlation of forces" -- and a consistent operational code of international conduct designed to advance the intentions of the Soviet Union have caused the United States to adopt what Soviet leaders call a more realistic policy.

Moscow's official newspaper, Pravda, said flatly on August 22, 1973, after the touted summits held in Moscow and Washington:

> Peaceful coexistence does not mean the end of the struggle of the two-world social system. The struggle between the proletariat and the bourgeoisie, between world socialism and imperialism, will be waged right up to the complete and final victory of communism on a world scale.[5]

This extraordinary frankness on the part of Soviet leaders seems to have escaped most U.S. observers, who would like to think that peaceful coexistence is the same as their concept of detente and will lead to "a generation of peace," as President Nixon promised.

On April 18, 1975, despite a formal peace accord concluded by the U.S. Secretary of State in 1973, communist troops were fighting their way to final victory in Vietnam. An authoritative Pravda editorial and a parallel Isvestia statement hailed detente as having brought about a "significant breakthrough" in "relations between the USSR and the U.S." Even the pre-eminent old Bolshevik theoretician, Mikhail Suslov, who spoke on April 16 at the CPSU's Plenum, suggested that capitalism was actually weakening.

Brezhnev, who died in 1982, was succeeded, in short order, by three men with different personalities and styles but the same ideological indoctrination. The Soviet world view, therefore, has been consistent down to the present day.

Mikhail Gorbachev, who took control of the CSPU on March 11, 1985, after the short reigns of Yuri Andropov and Konstantin Chernenko, has called for reforming the economy and allowing more outspoken criticism of government mistakes (glasnost). He has never, however, deviated from classical Leninist doctrines about the one-party state and its conflict with capitalist nations.

In his opening remarks to the Politburo upon accepting his post as General Secretary of the Communist Party, Gorbachev said:

> We will firmly adhere to the Leninist course of peace and peaceful coexistence. . . . We value the successes of relaxation of international tensions achieved in the 1970s. . . .

Gorbachev, emphasizing Soviet support of revolutionary class warfare against non-communist governments and aiding national wars of liberation from imperialists, continued:

> The Soviet Union has always backed the peoples' struggle for the liberation from colonial oppression. At present, as well, our sympathies are with the countries of Asia, Africa, and Latin America, which are marching along the road of strengthening independence and social renovation.[6]

In Gorbachev's words, there were variations of language calculated to alarm Western observers less than the blunt words of Brezhnev, but he echoed basic Soviet strategy, long established and well understood by CPSU leaders. He spoke forthrightly about "cherishing and strengthening in all ways fraternal friendship with our closest friends and allies -- countries of the great socialist community," i.e., the Soviet dominated communist nations. He went on to declare, "We will do our utmost to enhance the role and influence of socialism in world affairs," and then turned without hesitation to refer hostilely to the United States, inevitably cast in the role of the enemy. He implied that the American nation was responsible for the "terrible threat" of the arms race that "loomed so large and dark over mankind."

Some years hence, younger generations may have different ideas, but for the present this national strategy of fundamental hostility to the non-communist world provides the best clue there is to Soviet behavior in international affairs. Detente and glasnost are, and are likely to remain, fundamental elements of a strategy by which the USSR expects ultimately to gain total strategic superiority over the United States.

6

NOTES

1.   Lenin, V.I., <u>Selected Works</u> (New York: International Publishers, 1943), Vol. VIII, p. 282.

2.   Kohler, Foy D., Mose L. Harvey, <u>et. al.</u>, <u>Soviet Strategy for the Seventies: From the Cold War to Peaceful Coexistence</u> (Coral Gables, Florida: Center for Advanced International Studies, 1973), p. 28.

3.   Kohler, Foy D., <u>Soviet "Peaceful Coexistence" is Not Western Detente</u>, Hearings of the Subcommittee for Europe, House Committee on Foreign Affairs, May 15, 1974, p. 24.

4.   <u>Pravda</u>, December 22, 1972.

5.   <u>Ibid.</u>, August 22, 1973.

6.   <u>TASS</u>, March 11, 1985; also excerpts in <u>Washington Post</u>, March 12, 1985.

Chapter 2

NATURE OF SOVIET GLOBAL STRATEGY

Roger E. Kanet and James Arnold Miller

The Soviet Union is a global power, a nation with interests throughout the world and with growing capabilities and a <u>global strategy</u> to pursue these interests. A global strategy, or what some call a "grand strategy," may be defined as a comprehensive, coordinated, coherent, flexible, and long-range plan to advance national goals and objectives through the integrated employment of all the instruments of national power.

In essence, the Kremlin leaders believe that they must lead an unrelenting worldwide struggle until their system of socialism emerges victorious over the contradictory system of capitalism.

Soviet Strategic Thinking

While serving as Soviet Defense Minister in the early 1970s, Marshal A.A. Grechko spelled out the rationale for the universal struggle of socialism against capitalism, attributing to Lenin credit for developing most of the specific principles on which the current international behavior of the Soviet state is based:

> V.I. Lenin remarked that the one who wins a war is the one who possesses superiority in the economic, sociopolitical, scientific-technological, moral and military fields.
> V.I. Lenin pointed out the ever expanding and deepening ties between politics and war.[1]

From the outset, the Soviet state, created by Lenin in 1917, has approached all of its activities, domestic as well as international, in a holistic manner which explicitly and persistently takes into account all the major elements of organized human activity, e.g., military, economic, and political-ideological. From the Marxist-Leninist perspective, the central question of any analysis and evaluation of political or military conflict is its socio-political nature. "There are no two isolated kinds of policies. . . . Foreign and domestic policies are two aspects of the same policy."[2]

Warfare, which the Soviet leaders view as a regular occurrence, is caused in the contemporary world by the imperialist states. All recent wars have resulted from imperialist policy which has "aimed at obstructing the historical advance of the cause of national independence, democracy and socialism."[3]

In the official Soviet view, the struggle for peace is inseparable from the struggle for worldwide social change and progress. "World peace rules out wars between states as a means of attaining the goals of social reorganization, but preserves the field for the class struggle within an antagonistic society and for social revolution and national liberation."[4] Even in periods of peace, Soviet leaders continue their persistent efforts to wage this struggle through such means as propaganda, disinformation, subversion, espionage, and support for terrorism and wars of national liberation.

Although the Soviet leaders do not have a comprehensive and detailed master plan according to which they are attempting to conquer the world, they do have long-term objectives and aspirations that fit into an overall global strategy. When opportunities arise to accomplish portions of that strategy -- and when the risks and costs are not viewed as prohibitive -- the Soviet leaders are likely to attempt to take advantage of them.

According to General Jan Senja, Chief of Staff to the Czechoslovak Minister of Defense prior to his defection to the West in 1968, the USSR and its Warsaw Pact allies had developed a planning document entitled "The Long-Term Strategic Plan for the Next Ten to Fifteen Years and the Years After."[5] Senja maintained that the plan calls for the isolation of the main target, the United States, through the neutralization, or "Finlandization," of West Europe; reduction of Western political influence in and economic access to the raw-materials-rich developing countries; and the encouragement of insurgency in areas of strategic importance to the United States, such as Central America.[6] According to Senja, the strategic plan included Moscow's intentions to try, with the assistance of "progressive movements," to convince U.S. allies that military alliances were unnecessary.[7]

Senja noted that Moscow's strategic plan "is subject to constant revision to ensure that it takes into account new factors introduced by changes in the world's political forces and unforeseen advances in Western technology which necessitate Soviet arms control initiatives."[8]

It must be emphasized that the Soviet leaders insist that they are waging "war" against the capitalist world and that they have been committed, since the creation of the Soviet state, to using all means available to them to wage the incessant struggle until socialism emerges victorious over capitalism. Marxist-Leninists defined the war concept as:

> The essence of war is the continuation of politics by means of armed forces. This is the main characteristic of war. Therefore, this definition of the essence of war does not include many of the important ways that are used to secure victory in the war, notably economic, diplomatic and other forms of struggle.
>
> A full description of the content of war must contain the aggregate of social processes which in one way or another express the essence of the war and form part of it.
>
> In peacetime the chief role is generally played by non-violent means of policy-making, while violent means do not assume the character of a large-scale armed struggle, but in wartime the situation changes radically: means of mass armed violence move to the foreground.
>
> Economic and ideological struggle, open and secret diplomacy, and other forms of struggle, are used not only to further the armed struggle but also to supplement it, and in aggregate with it they are able to break the will of the enemy to resist, and thus secure victory.[9]

Not surprisingly, the Soviet approach to relations with socialist allies is also viewed as multidimensional. According to Marshal Grechko, relations with other socialist states are "determined by the very nature of socialist society and have firm sociopolitical, economic, ideological and military-strategic foundations."[10]

The multidimensional, integrated Soviet approach to politics has also been described very clearly by Major General Yu.Ya. Kirshin, a military intellectual writing for his peers, in an article published in 1982 entitled "World Politics: Essence, Basic Features and Trends." The general wrote:

> During the age of transition from capitalism to socialism, the struggle between the working class and the bourgeoisie has assumed the form of an interstate struggle between socialist and capitalist states which is constantly being waged in interconnected spheres: economic, political, and ideological.[11]

What is so significant about Kirshin's statement is that the view of interstate relations in time of peace that is presented here is quite different from the dominant view in the West, where compromise and cooperation between states are considered normal. In the Soviet perspective, all activities -- including trade relations, cultural exchanges, and arms control negotiations -- are part of the universal struggle between socialism and capitalism that will come to an end only with the final triumph of socialism over the capitalist system.

In addition to noting the multidimensional nature of the struggle against capitalism, Kirshin also pointed out that the "confrontation of the two social systems is a class struggle on a worldwide scale. . . . All political processes and events of greater or lesser significance which are taking place in the world are related to the main conflict of the age, and many of them arise from it." Kirshin then concludes that:

> A world strategic stage has been formed for the struggle between the two social systems. The front of the struggle between the socialist and capitalist states passes through the geographical plane -- through all regions and continents; through the economic plane -- in the competition and struggle in the sphere of economics; through the political plane -- in the confrontation of classes in the world arena; and through the ideological plane -- through the consciousness and hearts of the people.[12]

The Military Dimension of Soviet Global Strategy

Despite the multidimensional nature of Soviet global strategy, it has been the military dimension which has been most significant in expanding Soviet influence on the international scene.

Historically, military power has represented an essential instrument in the Soviet (and earlier Russian) pursuit of state interests. Given the historical relative backwardness of Russia and the Soviet Union and the relatively limited ability of Soviet leaders to exert substantial influence on world affairs through economic or political-ideological means alone, the maintenance and extension of military power has been viewed as essential to the overall interests of the Soviet state. Added to this is the importance of the traditional Russian and Soviet conception of security.

From the days of the Czars, Russian leaders have responded to a perceived security threat by means of a policy aimed at eliminating the source of the threat -- by expanding and absorbing the source of that threat, if possible. Directly related to this policy that might be called "defensive expansion" has been the desire to resist simultaneously all possible sources of threat to Russian/Soviet security. In the contemporary world, this means the ability to match simultaneously the military power of all potential opponents -- including the North Atlantic Treaty Organization (NATO) and the People's Republic of China.

The Soviet leadership has pursued a policy that has resulted in a disproportionate percentage of national income going into the military sector. On the one hand this has resulted in a massive military buildup over the past thirty years; on the other, it has led to substantially slowed growth in the civilian sector of the economy and major shortages of all sorts of basic goods and services.[13]

Given the centralized and authoritarian nature of Soviet society, however, these domestic economic problems have not resulted in pressures that would force the leadership to modify its policy of continued military buildup. By the mid-1980s the Soviet military controlled uniformed forces numbering more than five million (excluding more than one million border guards, security forces, and other paramilitary formations); it is estimated that military expenditures currently absorb 15 to 17 percent of the total Soviet gross national product (GNP).[14]

Over the past two decades, Soviet forces have steadily expanded and upgraded every category of weapons systems. Soviet ground force divisions have been reorganized, enlarged, and equipped with increasingly modern tanks, artillery, and helicopters. Soviet naval forces continue to receive larger and more capable ships and submarines. Soviet air forces are being modernized with high-performance aircraft. In addition to these force enhancements, Soviet military planners are adapting operations to the capabilities of new systems and changing political objectives as part of the dynamics of combined arms warfare.[15]

The centerpiece of Soviet military power is comprised of the Strategic Rocket Forces, which command almost 1,400 Intercontinental Ballistic Missile (ICBM) launchers and more than 900 Submarine-Launched Ballistic Missiles (SLBMs).

Soviet Ground Forces, which include 1.8 million men, have been upgraded significantly during the past two decades. Of 199 active tank, motorized rifle, and airborne divisions, 98 are positioned opposite NATO (including thirty in East Europe) and an additional 53 are located along the Sino-Soviet border and in the Soviet Far East.

The Soviet Army disposes of approximately 51,000 battle tanks, 34,000 artillery pieces, and an additional 70,000 armored personnel carriers and other military vehicles.

The Soviet Air Forces contain about 900 bombers, 6,100 fighter aircraft and fighter-bombers, and 600 transport planes.

Finally, Soviet Naval Forces continue to expand and include more than 2,250 surface and submarine vessels.[16]

Thus, Soviet military power performs a number of major functions for the Kremlin in its pursuit of global objectives. First,

it provides Moscow with an effective defensive umbrella beneath
which it has been able to pursue more actively than in the past
objectives outside traditional areas of Soviet domination, such as
East Europe. Secondly, the expansion of conventional military
capabilities has enabled the Soviet leadership to intervene directly
in a number of regional conflicts in ways that have had a major
impact on the outcome of those conflicts.[17] In addition -- and this
may well be the most important factor stemming from the
expansion of Soviet military power -- the Kremlin leaders have
attempted to use their recently developed military capabilities to
influence the policies of other countries.

The threat posed by Soviet nuclear weapons has been
important in promoting the antinuclear and nuclear-freeze
movements in the United States, Japan, and West Europe. In Europe
the growth of Soviet military power (for example, the installation of
intermediate-range SS-20 missiles targeted on West Europe), in the
view of many analysts, encouraged the West European peace
movements in their attempts to pressure Western governments not
to counter the Soviet SS-20 deployments by deploying cruise and
Pershing II missiles.[18]

Moreover, the growth of Soviet military power has most
probably played an important role in influencing West European
leaders to continue efforts to pursue a policy of detente, despite
growing evidence of expansionist Soviet policies in such areas as
Afghanistan, Sub-Saharan Africa, Central America, and Cambodia.

In Asia, the enormous expansion of Soviet military power may
have helped to influence the new Chinese leadership that a massive
increase in their own military spending is not worth the cost and
effort. Toward Japan, the Soviet leaders apparently have been
pursuing a policy -- unsuccessful so far -- aimed at intimidating the
Japanese into loosening their security ties with the United States.

In Africa it is primarily the use of military power that has
provided the Kremlin with the opportunity to expand the Soviet role
in such countries as Angola and Ethiopia. Cuban troops and Soviet
advisers transported to each of these countries in the 1970s assured
victories by pro-Soviet forces.

Soviet threats against the government of President Zia of
Pakistan, although not completely successful, have apparently
resulted in reduced and more cautious Pakistani support for the
Afghan resistance.

The growth of Soviet military power has been -- and continues
to be -- the single most important dimension of Soviet global
strategy. However, this dimension has been employed in conjunction
with other aspects of Soviet strategy. In Europe, for example, the
Soviet leadership has balanced the threat represented by its
expanding military power with promises of improved political
relations and expanding economic ties that will be mutually

beneficial to all parties. While the military dimension of Soviet strategy is the most important component of the USSR's overall global strategy, the leadership will continue to attempt to use it in conjunction with a broad range of other strategy instruments.

The Economic Dimension of Soviet Global Strategy

Despite significant weaknesses in the Soviet economy, the Kremlin leaders employ economic instruments in their global strategy. The system of central planning introduced in the USSR by Stalin results in an economic system in which all decisions concerning the allocation of investments, production, prices, and foreign trade are made by the central leadership. This system -- although it permits the concentration of resources to accomplish priority goals, e.g., the emphasis on military construction and relevant heavy industry, as well as the integration of economic activity into a unified approach to global strategy -- has also brought with it serious problems such as waste, inefficiency, and low levels of productivity.

After decades of high growth rates based primarily on extensive factors (an expanding work force and high levels of investments) Soviet economic growth has slowed appreciably during the past two decades. Despite twenty years of calls by the Soviet leadership to resolve these problems, the Soviet economy continues to lag far behind the economies of the West and Japan. The most important economic problems currently faced by the Soviet Union include the lack of investment capital and technology needed to open up the rich raw materials storehouse of Siberia, the continuing inability to develop and adapt modern technology to production, and shortages of a wide range of consumer goods (including agricultural products).

These factors have had a major impact on the way in which the economic dimension has influenced Soviet global strategy. In fact, in its relations with the industrialized states of the West and Japan, the Soviet leadership has pursued a policy over the course of the past fifteen years aimed at attempting to ameliorate its domestic economic problems. In part, at least, the demands of this policy have run counter to other Soviet objectives; in part, however, the Soviet leaders have also attempted to integrate their economic policy toward the industrialized states of the West into their overall objective of extending their own influence in world affairs.

The Soviet policy of detente of the 1970s was designed, among other things, to create an environment in which the USSR would be able to gain access to Western credits, and more important Western technology, as a means of resolving some of the problems mentioned above. For example, throughout the decade Moscow attempted to involve the Japanese in the exploitation of Siberian oil and gas reserves, and Moscow negotiated a wide array of economic agreements that brought to the USSR not only the products of Western technology, but also the technology and production processes themselves. Chemical plants, automobile and truck factories, and a host of other production facilities were constructed by Western firms as part of the expanded East-West economic cooperation that characterized the detente period.

Moreover, grain from the United States and several other major exporters provided the Soviet leadership with the ability to fulfill some of its commitments to the Soviet population without running the risks that they feared might come with economic reform. In return the USSR supplied the West with increasing amounts of petroleum and natural gas -- the only Soviet exports besides weapons and gold that were really competitive on the world market.

Soviet economic policy toward the West since about 1970 has had two clear objectives. First and foremost has been the goal of resolving Soviet domestic economic problems without the necessity of revamping the central planning or command structure of the economy. Related to this goal has been the attempt to establish economic ties with various Western states that would enable the Kremlin to bring economic pressure to bear on Western policies.

For example, the growing dependence of several West European states on Soviet oil and gas deliveries (although still relatively small) has brought with it the possibility of the USSR exerting economic pressure on those states to pursue policies compatible with Soviet interests. Although there is no evidence to date that the Soviet leaders have used their economic power for this purpose, a situation might arise in which they would use this potential influence on the political leadership of several West European states.

In addition to the possible Western dependence on Soviet energy, another aspect of Soviet economic relations with the West has been the overall importance of the Soviet market for the industrial exports of the West. Even though the USSR and its East European "partners" still absorb a relatively small percentage of the total exports of the industrialized states, the market represented by the Soviet Union and East Europe has been important to the West during the past decade of economic stagflation and high unemployment. Soviet spokesmen have continually emphasized, in their attempts to influence West Europe to continue the pursuit of policies of detente, the economic benefits that accrue to the West.

It is necessary to emphasize the relative weakness of the USSR's economic position in relations with the West. Although the Soviet leaders have attempted to use the expanded commercial relations with the countries of West Europe and Japan for purposes of influencing the overall policies of those countries toward the USSR, to date their own position has not been strong enough to accomplish more than a small percentage of their objectives. The domestic economic objective of solving the structural problems of the Soviet economy by importing Western technology has not really been achieved, despite the Soviet success in obtaining a broad range of Western technology over the course of the past fifteen years. In the realm of political goals, as Angela Stent has argued, the Kremlin has at least three sets of objectives in its economic relations with the West.[19]

A primary political object is to continue to strengthen the commitment to detente of the countries of West Europe and Japan and, if possible, to induce these countries to be more accommodating toward the interests of the Soviet Union, in return for expanding export markets for their industrial goods in the USSR.

A second objective, already mentioned above, is the creation of Western economic dependence on the USSR, e.g., in the area of energy -- which Moscow might later use to exert political pressures on Western governments.

A third objective relates to the long-term Soviet interest in dividing the United States from its allies in Europe and Asia. Since East-West trade has become far more important for the economies of West Europe and Japan than it has for the United States, differences in perception have emerged in the United States, West Europe and Japan concerning the benefits of that trade and concerning the rules under which such trade should occur.

In recent years the United States has taken a position that calls for greater restrictions on trade with the Soviet Union, while the West Europeans and Japanese have emphasized the overall benefits that expanded trade with the Soviet Union and East Europe has brought.[20] During the 1980s differences between the Reagan administration and the governments of major U.S. allies on trade policy toward the USSR have been a source of tension within the Western alliance system. The Soviet leaders clearly viewed that tension as beneficial to their long-term interests and have attempted to play on that tension.

In the Third World Moscow has attempted, ever since the mid-1950s, to use economic assistance and trade -- in conjunction with military and political relations -- to influence the domestic and foreign policies of developing countries.[21] In its global strategy, Moscow clearly recognizes the importance of the developing world for the economic welfare and security of the United States and its major allies. Especially noteworthy is the persisting effort of the Soviet leaders to improve their ability to cut off or disrupt the access of the United States, the NATO allies, and Japan to Third World sources of energy and non-fuel minerals which are so vital to modern nations.

It should be noted that weaknesses in the Soviet economy place limits on what can be achieved in the Third World. Although leaders in a number of developing states are attracted to the Soviet economic model and are committed to lessening their countries' dependence on the imperialist West, they have found that the USSR is not a particularly reliable economic partner. It can provide neither the investment capital nor the industrial products required by these countries. Thus, many of the most radical of Third World states (e.g., Angola, Ethiopia, and Mozambique) have continued to maintain -- and even to expand -- their economic ties with the West. However, despite the inability of Moscow to date to implement many of its economic objectives in the Third World, it continues to see the long-term disruption of close economic relations between key Third World states and the West as an important element in its global strategy.

The Political-Ideological Dimension of Soviet Global Strategy

The political-ideological sphere of Soviet strategy is of central importance to the Soviet leadership in its struggle to overcome capitalism. Activities included in the political-ideological dimension of Soviet policy include open and secret diplomacy; the use of front organizations; relations with other communist parties; promotion of Soviet objectives in the United Nations and other international bodies; propaganda and disinformation; and, covert activities such as assassination, espionage, and aid to terrorist groups.

In the Soviet view, expressed on numerous occasions by virtually all senior Soviet political leaders and analysts, "peaceful coexistence" or detente does not include an abatement of the global struggle against capitalism. An example of the political-ideological instrument of Soviet national power in operation to support overall Soviet strategy can be found in what political commentator V. Korionov in 1983 called the broadest cooperation on the part of communist parties with all political and social parties and groups in the West to oppose the deployment in West Europe of new U.S. intermediate-range missiles. According to Korionov:

> The peace initiatives put forward by the Soviet Union and other socialist countries are regarded . . . as a real alternative to the policy of armament buildup pursued by the United States and the NATO bloc with a view to achieving military superiority. Again and again communists fix the people's attention on the foremost task of 1983: that of preventing the deployment of new American nuclear missiles in Europe.

In NATO countries, including the United States, there is a growing awareness of the terrible danger inherent for mankind in the unprecedented arms race unleashed by the present Washington administration.[22]

This statement is illustrative of Soviet attempts to employ political propaganda in support of other aspects of their overall policy. This attempt follows directly from the Soviet view of the importance of the ideological struggle in determining the outcome of the conflict between communism and capitalism. This struggle "plays an enormous part in securing the support of the broad popular masses for politics and for war."[23]

Throughout the past decade, or more, the Soviet leadership has attempted to play on Western concerns about the dangers of continued high levels of tension in East-West relations. At the Twenty-fifth Congress of the Communist Party of the Soviet Union in February 1976, Leonid Brezhnev underscored the Soviet conception of the meaning of detente, stating: "We make no secret of the fact that we see detente as the way to create more favorable conditions for peaceful socialist and Communist construction."[24]

Similarly in an article in Pravda a year earlier it was argued that peaceful coexistence "is essentially a class policy conducive to the strengthening of the position and prestige of the socialist countries, while undermining the aggressive imperialist forces and narrowing their opportunities for plotting against the cause of peace and social progress."[25]

In the Third World, Soviet ideological and political initiatives have had as their primary purpose undermining the existing relationships between the developing countries and the West. Throughout the Third World the Kremlin leadership has identified itself with the aspirations for independence and development of the leaderships of the developing states, while picturing the United States and the countries of West Europe as the primary source of those countries' problems.

An important aspect of the USSR's political-ideological struggle against the West has been Moscow's involvement in supporting terrorist and other low-intensity conflict activities. The evidence on the relationship between the Soviet Union and a host of terrorist organizations is now conclusive.[26] Even though Moscow does not have direct control over most of the terrorist groups active today, it does supply massive amounts of arms and money to the revolutionary forces involved in terrorist activities. As Roberta Goren has concluded in her excellent historical survey of Soviet support for international terrorism:

Since 1917, the Soviet Union has consistently, although not always successfully, attempted to change the 'correlation of forces' by implementing the terrorist option. . . . This remains very much part of the doctrinal focus of the Soviet government. The measure of its success in the last fifteen years is the fact that so far the West has refused to face the implications of this aspect of Soviet policy.[27]

In its direct and indirect support for terrorist activities, Moscow expects that the ultimate targets of the terrorist groups -- even if those groups cannot be controlled from Moscow -- are likely to be the United States, West Europe, and Japan. In the long run, terrorist activities, in particular those carried out inside Western states, are expected to contribute to the gradual erosion and gradual weakening of capitalist society.

Continuing Limitations on Soviet Globalism

In spite of the significant expansion of Soviet capabilities in recent years and the new role that the USSR is now able to play in international affairs, its power and influence are still limited. First of all, the new Soviet position in Asia and Africa depends heavily on the coincidence of Soviet interests with those of "client" states. The expulsion of the Soviet presence from both Egypt and Somalia during the 1970s indicates the degree to which Moscow depends on the goodwill of such client states.

Second, even with large-scale Soviet support some Third World states have been unable to accomplish the primary goal of creating a stable political system. In Angola, for example, ten years of Soviet and Cuban support have not yet resulted in the elimination of major domestic opposition to the Popular Movement for the Liberation of Angola (MPLA). The government would collapse without the continued support of its communist allies. Recently, Mozambique has negotiated a security arrangement with the government of the Republic of South Africa and has turned to West Europe for financial support because of the inability or unwillingness of Moscow to expand its commitments.

Another example of the inability of the Soviet leaders to accomplish their goals -- at least more than partially -- has been in Afghanistan. The inability of Taraki, and later Amin, to consolidate their rule in Afghanistan during 1978 and 1979 eventually resulted in the Soviet decision to intervene directly in 1979. Despite the introduction of massive military power the USSR has not succeeded, after more than six years, in eliminating widespread opposition to the puppet regime of Babrak Karmal.

Moreover, the Soviet invasion and continued military presence in Afghanistan resulted in substantial condemnation, even from developing countries, which in the past generally supported the

Soviet Union. Perhaps the most important long-term cost of the Soviet invasion of Afghanistan has been the evidence that it provided to leaders of developing states of the expansionist nature of the Soviet state.

Elsewhere in the Middle East, Moscow was largely frozen out of the major developments in the Arab-Israeli conflict for more than a decade after the October War of 1973. Only by committing themselves to the support of the members of the Rejectionist Front in the late 1970s were they able to continue to play a role -- albeit quite marginal -- in developments in the region. However, that role was played largely on terms set by the Arabs.

Dependence on Moscow did not prevent Syria from intervening in the Lebanese Civil War of 1975-76, contrary to Soviet wishes at that time. Nor did Soviet displeasure prevent Iraq, which depended almost entirely on Soviet weapons until its efforts in the late 1970s to diversify its sources, from invading Iran in the fall of 1980. Even events in Lebanon and in Syria since 1983 indicate that, although the USSR provides virtually all the military hardware and substantial numbers of military advisers for Syria, President Assad's government continues to make its decisions largely independent of Soviet wishes.

The ouster of the Soviet- and Cuban-backed communist regime on the Caribbean island of Grenada in October 1983 represented a clear setback for Soviet strategy in Latin America. However, since then the Soviet leaders have not reduced, but rather increased, their support to their Cuban and Nicaraguan proxies.

When we turn to the position of the Soviet Union in the international communist movement we find the most serious challenges to its expanded role in the international system. Despite successive changes in Soviet leadership since 1982 and a major shift in Chinese domestic and foreign policy, Soviet relations with China have not improved significantly over the past decade. The Chinese continue to represent a threat to Soviet interests in Asia, and the Chinese have been among the most vocal critics of detente with the Soviet Union and of Soviet expansion throughout the Third World. Evidence of the likelihood of greater Chinese cooperation -- even in the military realm -- with the United States, Japan, and West Europe is viewed with great alarm in Moscow.

In Europe the growth of national communism, especially in Italy and Spain, has challenged the dominance of the Soviet position within the European communist movement. An even greater threat was presented by the revolutionary convulsions that seized communist Poland in the Solidarity period. Although the imposition of martial law and the normalization that followed it have at least temporarily stifled the overt challenge to the Polish communist system, they have not dealt with the fundamental underlying causes of that challenge.

In the global military realm, the deployment of intermediate-range nuclear missiles by NATO during the past several years and the revitalization of U.S. military capabilities by the Carter administration and -- even more vigorously -- by the Reagan administration, have presented Soviet leaders with a whole new series of problems. Unless the Soviet leadership is willing either to negotiate seriously on limitations and reductions in nuclear weapons or to expend an increasing percentage of its GNP on armaments, it will be faced with the prospect of falling behind the United States.

Besides the external factors that are likely to restrict the expansion of the Soviet role in world affairs, the continuing weakness of the Soviet economy has limited the degree to which the USSR can compete effectively with the West in influencing international economic developments. To date, the USSR has been required to adapt itself to the existing international economic system as a means of participating in world trade. Soviet economic relations with both the West and the developing countries occur in an international economic system dominated by the Western industrial countries. In fact, the growth of East-West economic relations during the 1970s created a certain degree of interdependence of the two groups of countries. The USSR and its East European allies have discovered that they are no longer immune to developments in the international economy such as inflation or recession.

It is not likely that the Kremlin will be able in the coming years to solve the basic structural problems of the Soviet economy. In addition, the probability of increasing difficulty in meeting Soviet growing energy needs (and the needs of their East European allies) bodes ill for high growth rates. With the greater likelihood of a continued slowdown in economic growth rates, the Soviet leaders will find it difficult to make additional commitments of the sort that they have already made to Cuba, Vietnam, Angola, Ethiopia, and Afghanistan.

Yet, having noted the problems that the Soviet leaders continue to face in their attempts to extend their global influence and to affect events in regions both near to and far from their own borders, it must be noted that the power base from which the Gorbachev regime is able to operate in world affairs is substantially stronger than that which Khrushchev inherited from Stalin in 1953 or that which Brezhnev took over from Khrushchev eleven years later.

Most important is the fact that the Kremlin leaders have devoted major efforts to building up both nuclear strategic and conventional military capabilities and have demonstrated over the course of the past fifteen years or so that they are willing to employ that enhanced military power in a variety of ways and in conjunction with other capabilities in the attempt to accomplish their objectives. Limitations still exist on the ability of the USSR to act globally -- but the availablility of extensive military capabilities has enabled the leaders in the Kremlin to challenge Western interests throughout the world in ways that would have been unthinkable only twenty years ago.

Conclusion

Although the Soviet leaders have attempted to integrate all aspects of their foreign relations ever since the days of Lenin and Stalin, it has only been during the past two decades that they have developed the capabilities to permit them to project power on a global scale. Today the USSR possesses the capabilities (primarily military) that permit it to compete effectively for influence in world affairs. To what extent the Kremlin leaders will continue to be able to expand their role in the international system will depend to a large extent on the response of other actors in the system -- those in the West as well as those in the Third World -- and on developments within the Soviet Union itself. A persistent Western policy of non-reaction, combined with attitudes in the developing world that continue to view the West as the principal opponent, would permit the Kremlin to expand its relative ability to influence international developments on a global scale.

Despite disagreements within the Western alliance, the 1980s have witnessed a growing concern about Soviet expansionism and the beginnings of efforts to counter that expansion. The continued modernization of NATO forces and the deployment of U.S. intermediate-range missiles in Europe despite substantial opposition, the increasing disclosures about the Soviet involvement with international terrorism, the disillusionment of several Third World clients with the USSR's inability to provide true development assistance, and the impact of the Soviet efforts to conquer Afghanistan, the persistent malaise of the Soviet economy, and the fissures within the Soviet empire (in particular in East Europe) -- all of these developments probably have reduced Soviet optimism.

Yet Soviet nuclear and conventional military capabilities continue to expand, and Moscow's abilites to influence events in the Third World continue to increase, despite setbacks here and there. The Western alliance is still divided, not only concerning the most appropriate approach for dealing with the multidimensional Soviet threat, but also concerning issues such as intra-alliance economic and military relations. Furthermore, important issues alienate much of the developing world from the United States and its allies.

What success the Soviet leadership has in the future in pursuing its strategy aimed at expanding its worldwide influence will depend, to a significant degree, on the ability of the West to unite in (1) developing a Western or Free World global strategy in response to the global and multidimensional challenge to Western interests presented by the Soviet Union, and, (2) resolving some of its outstanding problems with key Third World states. Without such a unified approach on the part of the West the Soviet leaders will continue to find opportunities to pursue successfully the global strategy outlined above.

NOTES

1. Marshal A.A. Grechko, The Armed Forces of the Soviet State (Moscow, 1975; translated and published under the auspices of the United States Air Force) (Washington: U.S. Government Printing Office, n.d.), p. 252. For an excellent study of Marxist-Leninist views of international relations see V. Kubalkova and A.A. Cruickshank, Marxism-Leninism and the Theory of International Relations (London: Routledge & Kegan Paul, 1980), especially pp. 212-232.

2. Marxism-Leninism on War and Army (Moscow: Progress Publishers, 1972); published under the auspices of the United States Air Force (Washington: U.S. Government Printing Office, 1974), pp. 8-9.

3. Ibid., p. 15.

4. F.M. Burlatskiy, "The Philosophy of Peace," Voprosy Filosifii, no. 12 (December 1982); translated and excerpted in Strategic Review, Vol. 2, no. 3 (1983), p. 82.

5. Jan Senja, We Will Bury You (London: Sidgwick and Jackson, 1982), pp. 101-108, 153-154.

6. Ibid.

7. Ibid., p. 108. Observers in the West have questioned the validity of some of what Senja, a defector, has had to say. Even if part of Senja's testimony is fabricated, the fact remains that Soviet behavior in recent decades is sufficient proof that the Soviet leaders are proceeding along the general lines pointed out by Senja.

8. Senja, Op. cit., p. 101.

9. Marxism-Leninism on War and Army, pp. 10-11.

10. Grechko, The Armed Forces of the Soviet State, p. 329.

11. Major General Yu.Ya. Kirshin, "World Politics: Essence, Basic Features and Trends," Voprosy Filosofil, no. 12 (1982); translated and excerpted in Strategic Review, Vol. 11, no. 3 (1983), pp. 82-83.

12. Ibid., p. 83.

13. For a discussion of the economic implications of the Soviet military burden see Myron Rush, "Impact and Implications of Soviet Defense Spending," in Soviet Politics in the 1980s, ed. Helmut Sonnenfeldt (Boulder, CO: Westview Press, 1985), pp. 131-145.

14. U.S. Department of Defense, Soviet Military Power 1985 (Washington: U.S. Government Printing Office, 1985), p. 10.

15. Ibid., p. 14.

16. Ibid., p. 26. This and the following information on Soviet military capabilities is taken from Soviet Military Power and from International Institute for Strategic Studies, The Military Balance, 1984-1985 (London: International Institute for Strategic Studies, 1984).

17. See Bruce D. Porter, The USSR and Third World Conflicts:

Soviet Arms and Diplomacy in Local Wars, 1945-1980 (Cambridge: Cambridge University Press, 1984).

18. For a discussion of this point see Gerhard Wettig, "East-West Security Relations at the Eurostrategic Level," Soviet Foreign Policy and East-West Relations, ed. Roger E. Kanet (New York: Pergamon, 1982), pp. 56-76.

19. See Angela Stent, "Economic Strategy," in Soviet Strategy Toward Western Europe, eds. Edwina Moreton and Gerald Segal (London-Boston: George Allen & Unwin, 1984), pp. 219-220.

20. John P. Hardt and Kate S. Tomlinson, "Soviet Economic Policies in Western Europe," in Soviet Policy in Western Europe: Implications for the Atlantic Alliance, ed. Herbert J. Ellison (Seattle-London: University of Washington Press, 1983), p. 188.

21. See for example, Roger E. Kanet, "Soviet Policy Toward the Developing World: The Role of Economic Assistance and Trade," The Soviet Union and the Developing Countries: Successes and Failures, ed. Robert H. Donaldson (Boulder, CO: Westview Press, 1981), pp. 331-357.

22. V. Korionov, "Stand Up Firmly for Each Other," Pravda, May 2, 1983; excerpted in Strategic Review, Vol. IX, no. 4 (1983), pp. 82-83.

23. A.S. Milovidov and V.G. Kozlov, eds., The Philosophical Heritage of V.I. Lenin and Problems of Contemporary War. (Moscow, 1972); translated and published under the auspices of the United States Air Force (Washington: U.S. Government Printing Office, 1975), pp. 215-216.

24. L.I. Brezhnev, Report to the 24th Congress of the Communist Party of the Soviet Union, March 30, 1976.

25. Y. Tarabrin, "Africa in Confrontation with U.S. Imperialism," International Affairs (Moscow), no. 6 (1975), p. 33.

26. Three important contributions to the growing literature on Soviet support for terrorism are: Claire Sterling, The Terror Network: The Secret War of International Terrorism (New York: Holt, Rinehart, Winston, 1981); Ray S. Cline and Yonah Alexander, Terrorism: The Soviet Connection (New York: Crane, Russak & Co., 1984); and Roberta Goren, The Soviet Union and Terrorism (London-Boston: George Allen & Unwin, 1984).

27. Goren, The Soviet Union and Terrorism, pp. 198-199.

Chapter 3

SOVIET CONCEPTUAL FRAMEWORK FOR
THE DEVELOPMENT AND APPLICATION OF MILITARY POWER

Phillip A. Petersen

Any attempt to construct the Soviet conceptual framework for the development and application of military power should begin with Soviet force structure itself. The Soviet armed forces include five separate forces: (1) the Strategic Rocket Forces (SRF); (2) the ground forces; (3) the air forces (Voyenno-Vozdushneyye Sily) or VVS; (4) the air defense forces (Voyska PVO); and (5) the naval forces. All except the naval forces are commonly included under the generic term "Soviet Army." While each of the five forces (sometimes referred to in the West as services) has a Commander-in-Chief (CINC) who is also a Deputy Minister of Defense, the CINCs do not have direct operational control over their forces. Their duties as CINC of their respective force involves essentially supervision of technical affairs and research and development. Each of the forces also has a Main Staff, which execute the role of coordinating, planning, and maintaining liaison with the armed forces General Staff.

To control the armed forces, the territory of the Soviet Union has been divided into military districts (MDs). Although the number of MDs has varied since they were first established by the Soviet government in 1918, today there are sixteen: Leningrad, Baltic, Belorussia, Carpathia, Odessa, Transcaucasus, Moscow, Kiev, North Caucasus, Volga, Ural, Central Asia, Turkestan, Siberia, Transbaykal, and Far East.[1] "Each military district is the highest military and administrative unification of units, formations, institutions of military education, institutions of various types of the armed forces and local registration and mobilization organs (military committees) which are located in a given territory"[2] of the Soviet state.

The Soviet Union also has groups of forces stationed outside its territory: (1) the Northern Group of Forces (NGF) in Poland; (2) the Central Group of Forces (CGF) in Czechoslovakia; (3) the Southern Group of Forces (SGF) in Hungary; and (4) the Group of

Soviet Forces, Germany (GSFG). While the USSR has troops in the Mongolian People's Republic, they function as part of the Soviet Forces in the Far East. In addition, "in the seas surrounding its borders the Soviet Union has created various fleets and flotillas."[3]

In a conflict, the groups of Soviet forces, fleets and flotillas, and forces in the MDs would be organized into formations to execute operations independent of the administrative structure. However, while forces may depart a military district as battlefield operations progress, the MD structure would be retained to serve as a principal wartime administrative entity.

Soviet Military Doctrine

Military doctrine is a highly developed discipline in the Soviet Union and constitutes a sophisticated framework for the examination of questions concerning military force employment and weapon systems development. It is formulated at the highest levels of Soviet political and military leadership. Military doctrine provides both the accepted view on the nature of future conflicts, as well as guidance for the military to follow in preparing the armed forces for war. Thus, military doctrine is an expression of the political policy of the Communist Party of the Soviet Union (CPSU) as reflected in the military policy of the Soviet government or, as Soviet writers put it, a directive of political strategy. It is distinguished from military science (see below) in that doctrine is a unified system of views and a guide to action elaborated and adopted by the state.[4]

Military doctrine interacts with strategy in that "strategy implements doctrine directly, and is its instrument in the elaboration of war plans and the preparation of the country for war."[5]

> In wartime, military doctrine drops into the background somewhat, since in armed combat, we are guided primarily by military-political and military-strategic considerations, conclusions and generalizations which stem from the conditions of the specific situation. Consequently, war, armed combat, is governed by strategy, not doctrine.[6]

As openly admitted, "Soviet military doctrine is offensive in character."[7]

Lieutenant General P. Zhilin explained that,

> naturally when we speak of the defensive nature of Soviet military doctrine we have in mind its political purpose -- which is the defense of the socialist Fatherland. It must not

be confused with the principles of Soviet military art which is characterized by active and decisive combat operations and military actions based on the same interest of defending the Homeland.[8]

If the Soviet Union is attacked or about to be attacked, it will wage war "in the most offensive fashion in order to bring about the rapid defeat of (its) enemies."[9] Clearly,

the Soviet doctrine of war does recognize the defensive laws and actions at strategic, operational, and tactical levels. But defense is considered a forced form of military action. Defense is assumed only when the forces and means are not sufficient to attack or when gaining time may become necessary for concentrating forces and providing favorable conditions to initiate a decisive offensive operation.[10]

Soviet military science includes the following principal components: the general theory (general principles of military science); the theory of military art; the theory of military development; military geography; and the theory of command and control. Within each of the theories of military science there exists an independent discipline dealing with its naval aspects. Collectively, the naval disciplines have been referred to as the "theory of the Navy."[11] The general theory of military science defines the interdependent and joint subordination of the relatively independent branches and disciplines within the military field. "It studies in general terms the means and possibilities of armed combat, its condition and special features."[12]

Soviet military art is defined as "the theory and practice of preparing for and conducting military operations on land, at sea, and in the air."[13] Military art includes the theory of strategy, operational art, and tactics, each of which represent a whole field of knowledge. All three are, however, interrelated, interdependent, and supplement each other. Among the three, strategy plays the predominant role.

"Strategy is a division of military art which investigates the principles of preparing for, and waging, war as a whole, and its campaigns."[14] In its applied aspect, it is concerned with the immediate preparation for war of the country's territory and combat theaters, specifically relating to the execution of strategic attack, strategic defense, and other types of military operations on a strategic scale.[15] "Strategic operations are the basic means for achieving the political goals of war."[16] Thus in evaluating the strategic content of war, the Soviet military believes that war is a complex system of interrelated, large, simultaneous, and successive strategic operations.[17] The relationship to political policy is said by the Soviet theoreticians to be "conditioned by the essence of war as a continuation of the politics of classes and governments by violent means."[18]

Within the Soviet framework for the application of military power, the theory of military art is structured so as to provide an operational guide for conducting those activities which support higher level requirements. Thus, "stemming from strategic requirements, operational art determines methods of preparing for and conducting operations to achieve strategic goals, and it gives the initial data for tactics."[19]

In essence, "operational art is the connecting link between strategy and tactics."[20] It encompasses the problems of preparing and conducting joint and independent operations by operational-strategic, operational, and operational-tactical field forces of the services for the Soviet armed forces.[21] Tactics concerns the refined laws and principles of actual combat, most often used in conjunction with the operations by military forces at the division level and lower.[22]

Military Geography

Military geography is that branch of military science dealing with political, economic, natural, and military conditions in various countries and theaters of military action from the viewpoint of their effect on the preparation for, and conduct of military operations. Military geography includes naval geography as an independent discipline within its boundaries.[23]

The broadest concept in military geography seems to be that of the theater of war or T.W. (teatr voiny or T.V.). Theater of war "is the term given to vast areas of land, sea, and air, prepared in a political, economic, and military sense, on which bilateral hostilities are conducted between two states or coalitions."[24] Thus, although the boundaries of theaters of war are established in peacetime, during the course of hostilities they may stretch to several continents or even over the whole globe.[25]

The territorial structure of the Soviet economy and its region-oriented organization is directly connected to the country's military-administrative system, that is, the country's division into military districts.[26] These military districts may be visualized as comprising four regional groups more or less analogous to the strategic rear and the rears of the potential theaters of war:

o   regions of the center, Volga area, and Ural area in the middle of the European part of the country (the strategic rear of the country);

o   regions of the Northwest, West, and Southwest along the Soviet Union's Western border (the rear of the Western T.W.);

o   regions of the South along the Southern borders of the country (the rear of the Southern T.W.); and

o   regions of the East (the rear of the Far Eastern T.W.).[27]

While the Soviet military leaders recognize the concept of a theater of war as a useful way to identify general areas of potential conflict and to prepare them for the event of hostilities, they focus their operational planning at the level of a theater of military action (TMA or in Russian teatr voennykh deistvii abbreviated TVD). Theaters of war may incorporate one or several TMAs.[28] The concept of a theater of military action has, understandably, evolved over time. Europe, for example, was considered to be a single theater of action in the 1960s but, by the mid-1970s, the Soviet instructors were teaching Voroshilov General Staff Academy students that Europe had been divided into three continental theaters of military action.[29]

During the mid-to-late 1970s, the Soviet military continued to work out the most appropriate geographical approach to strategic planning. Near Eastern, Middle Eastern, Northwestern, and Northern theaters of military action appeared and disappeared as strategic planning contingencies. Apparently, the first two were eventually subsumed in the Southern theater of military action, and the latter two into the Far Eastern theater of action.[30]

Even the definition of the TMA has been an issue of bureaucratic contention. By arguing for independent "sea" theaters of military action, the Navy could hope to obtain additional resources and avoid subordinating some of its fleets to the operational control of commanders in continental TMAs. That this persistent effort has been resolved by a narrower definition for the TMA is reflected in the 1983 Military Encyclopedic Dictionary which has defined the TMA simply as that part of the territory of a continent with the coastal waters of the oceans, internal seas and the air space above them (continental TMA); or the water areas of an ocean, including its islands, the contiguous coastlines of continents and the air space above them (oceanic TMA), within the boundaries of which are deployed strategic groupings of the armed forces and within which military operations are conducted.[31]

Based on a Soviet assessment, "the following have become the basic hallmarks of the TMA: its relative integrity in political and economic relations, the presence of objects of strategic importance on its territory and the potential for the deployment and the operations of the strategic groupings of armed forces."[32] In fact, "the preparation of a TMA, which is conducted according to a certain plan already in peacetime and is perfected in war, has important significance for the actions of troops (naval forces)."[33]

In peacetime, construction of land transportation routes, airfields, naval bases, pipelines, fixed systems for detection of submarines, and other kinds of infrastructure are planned, budgeted, and conducted under the rubric of the "preparation for war" of the TMA involved.[34] If hostilities approach, troops (naval forces) are to be mobilized and deployed on a TMA basis. War plans setting out the strategic operations for each TMA would be executed with the onset of hostilities. "In the course of such an operation each front (fleet) can conduct two or more operations in succession, with brief pauses and even without pauses."[35]

It should be noted that the largest Soviet maneuver formation is the front. It is an operational and administrative unit with size and composition subject to wide variation depending on the mission and situation. Generally considered to be roughly equivalent to a U.S./NATO army group, a front is usually composed of three to five maneuver armies and one or two air armies.

Forces organic or attached to a front could include artillery, missile, air defense, engineer, chemical, signal, intelligence, reconnaissance, and rear service units, plus airborne, air assault, airmobile, and special purpose forces.[43] The mission of a front offensive would be to seize key political and economic centers and concurrently destroy the enemy military forces defending them.[45]

Besides recognizing three continental theaters of military action in Europe (Northwestern, Western, and Southwestern TMAs) along with the Southern and Far Eastern TMAs, the USSR also recognizes North America, South America, Australia, Africa, and Antarctica as individual theaters of action.[36]

The Oceanic TMAs include the Atlantic, Pacific, Indian, and Arctic Oceans.[37] The Northwestern TMA includes Finland, Sweden, Norway, the Barents Sea, the Norwegian Sea, the North Sea, and the northern part of the Baltic Sea.

The Western TMA includes Denmark, the Federal Republic of Germany, the Netherlands, Belgium, Luxembourg, France, Great Britain, Spain, Portugal, Switzerland, Ireland, northern Morocco and western Algeria, Poland, the German Democratic Republic, Czechoslovakia, the southern part of the Baltic Sea, and the western part of the Mediterranean Sea.

The Southwestern TMA includes the eastern part of Turkey, Iran, Saudia Arabia, Syria, Iraq, Israel, Jordan, Lebanon, eastern Egypt, Afghanistan, Pakistan, India, Bangladesh, the eastern part of the Black Sea, and the Caspian Sea.

The Far Eastern TMA includes China, Mongolia, the Republic of Korea, Burma, Indochina (excluding Indonesia), Japan, the Philippines, Alaska, and Northern and Central Siberia.[38]

Although official charts attempt to represent what appears to be the present Soviet geographical approach to strategic planning, it is artificial in that "the boundaries of TMAs can be fixed or variable; they can be adjacent or they can overlap."[39] For example, the boundaries of theaters of military action in Europe can overlap. Threats to Warsaw Pact forces operating in Denmark and the Danish straits may require that combat actions be directed against southern Norway and Sweden by Pact forces in the Western TMA.

On the other hand, forces operating along the common flank in the Western and Southwestern theaters of military action may find operational necessity driving either a resubordination of some forces or a shifting of boundary lines during the course of the conduct of their respective strategic operations.

Within each theater of military action there are one or more strategic napravleniye, which may be translated as direction, sector, or axis. A stratetgic direction consists of a wide strip of land or sea, and the airspace above it, leading the armed forces of one warring party to the other's most important administrative-political and industrial-economic centers.[40]

Strategic directions involve operational-strategic maneuvers, which are undertaken by a combination of fronts, independent armies, or flotillas. Thus "a strategic sector usually permits operations by many strategic formations of various services."[41] Strategic directions, in turn, consist of one or more operational directions. An operational direction is a zone of terrain, water, or airspace, and sometimes a combination of these, within which an operational-strategic or operational formation conducts its operations.[42] Within the context of the continental TMA in which they lie, operational directions may be internal or coastal.

The Soviet military designates two types of maneuver armies. While both types are actually combined-arms organizations, a Soviet combined-arms army will normally have a preponderance of motorized rifle divisions, while a tank army will have a preponderance of tank divisions. An army is usually comprised of three to six divisions that also have a combined-arms structure. There are currently more than 180 Soviet maneuver divisions: more than 126 motorized rifle divisions, 47 tank divisions, and 7 airborne divisions.[44]

The Soviet military probably would hope that an initial strategic direction in the Western theater of military action, incorporating anywhere from two to four operational directions, would quickly break into two strategic directions. The northern strategic direction against Denmark and the Danish straits would involve one operational direction aimed at Jutland, and another representing the assault operation directed at seizing control of the Danish straits. On the southern flank of the Western TMA, Warsaw Pact forces moving up the Danube Valley might initially be an element of the forces of the Southwestern TMA which would, upon operational success, become resubordinated as an element of the forces of the Western TMA, or any such Danube front might well be made an element of the forces of the Western TMA right from the beginning of a conflict.

The Southwestern TMA could have as many as three initial strategic directions in a war against NATO. The specific number of strategic directions would, obviously, depend upon whether fighting were occurring in both the Western and Southwestern theaters of action. If a crisis in the Southwestern TMA arose in which the USSR could successfully avoid the outbreak of fighting in central Europe, it could well expect that the Greeks or the Turks would not intervene, thereby limiting Soviet operations in this event to a single strategic direction. In addition, the Turkish border with the Soviet Union is not considered by Soviet planners to lie in the same theater of military action as the Bosporus and Dardanelles. This fact apparently reflects at least two Soviet considerations: 1) any Soviet conflict with Pakistan and Iran could involve the United States and Turkey, but not necessarily NATO as an alliance; and 2) in an operational sense, combat actions against the Bosporus and Dardanelles would not involve the coordination of front boundaries with combat action against Eastern Turkey. The military geographical construct of the Southern TMA constitutes almost perfect symmetry.

In the Northwestern TMA, the initial offensive strategic direction against the Nordic countries would center upon the operational direction aimed at Finland and Denmark. If necessary, a defensive operational direction aimed at southern Finland could become a second offensive operational direction within this initial strategic direction.

Even though the Western TMA is considered by the Warsaw Pact to be the "main" theater of action,[46] a protracted conflict could necessitate the creation of a second strategic direction in the Northwestern TMA aimed at southern Norway and Sweden utilizing forces of the Western TMA. This second strategic direction in the Northwestern TMA could involve at least two operational directions. Forces operating within this second strategic direction would probably be resubordinated upon link-up of the forces operating on the two strategic directions of the Northwestern TMA.

At the other end of the Soviet Union, the Soviets apparently envision four strategic directions in the Far East: 1) against the Urimqi Military Region; 2) against the Shenyang and Beijing Military Regions; 3) against Japan, Korea, and the Philippines; and 4) against Alaska. Of these four strategic directions in the Far Eastern TMA, the direction against Northeast China constitutes the fulcrum of any successful strategic operation in the TMA and is, by far, the most complex of the possible strategic directions. This latter strategic direction is comprised of at least three initial operational directions, involving offensive operations by at least three fronts: 1) the Second Far Transbaikal front against the Beijing Region; 2) the Second Far Eastern front against northern Shenyang Military Region, and 3) the First Far Eastern front against eastern Shenyang Military Region.

Command and Control

The USSR has developed a comprehensive theory of command and control that corresponds to Moscow's highly structured view of military geography.[47] At the top the Defense Council (sovet oborony) unifies the military and civilian leadership so as to insure centralized political direction of military efforts. Immediately under the Defense Council, a Supreme High Command or SHC (verkhovnoe glavnokomandovanie or VKG) would direct strategic operations that could lead to radical changes in the military-political situation and the course of a war. The General Staff, serving as an executive agent for the Headquarters, Supreme High Command (stavka verkhovnogo glavnokomandovaniya), would insure the development and execution of a unified military strategy for the strategic and operational-strategic commands. To facilitate its ability to monitor events at the front, the General Staff would maintain representatives down to division level.

Until recently, for peacetime planning purposes the next level down in the command hierarchy was apparently the front. Up until the mid-1970s, the Soviet leaders certainly recognized that once war had begun they would have to establish some form of regional intermediate-level command to provide local control over groups of fronts in some areas.[48] During the Second World War, the Soviet military accomplished this by means of three different command variants: (1) the use of HQ, SHC representatives (such as G.K. Zhukov) to coordinate the operations of one or more fronts; (2) the creation of High Commands for strategic directions or theaters of military action; and (3) the use of HQ, SHC representatives to provide specific advice in their field of specialization (such as on the conduct of an air operation).[49]

This historical experience has influenced contemporary Soviet practice as shown in First Deputy Minister of Defense Sokolov's role as the equivalent of a HQ, SHC representative first in Ethiopia, then for air and ground operations against the Mujahideen in Afghanistan, and also in the appointment of the present CINC of the Soviet Ground Forces Petrov and then subsequently Army General V.L. Govorov as Commander-in-Chief of Troops in the Far East.

It was generally expected through the 1960s that in any major war the strategic direction would be the most likely level in the scale of military geography at which High Commands would have been established.[50] However, by the mid-1970s, then Chief of the General Staff Marshal Kulikov (he is now CINC, Warsaw Pact) led an initiative to make two important changes in Soviet thinking about wartime strategic leadership. First, he strongly favored the TMA over the Strategic Direction as the more appropriate level for establishment of High Commands. Second, he concluded that "the system of strategic leadership must be thought out, worked out and coordinated in all its details ahead of time, before the beginning of a war."[51]

His successor, Marshal Nikolay Ogarkov, strongly reaffirmed and refined Kulikov's initiative. Asserting not only that the principal operation in the war of today would be the strategic operation in a theater of military action, Ogarkov likewise stressed that preparation for war must be done in "time of peace" to ensure "the success of the organized introduction of the armed forces into the war and the destruction of the enemy."[52] One may also conclude that these High Commands would not be hastily assembled and organized after the war has begun, but that the commanders and staff have already been identified and exercised in peacetime.

Within the TMA, each front would move along an operational direction while armies subordinate to front formations would move along zones of advance, as would their subordinate divisions. Normally, "forces not in contact" are referred to as "second echelon forces." Even when those with a "larger view" contemplate the greater technical means at the disposal of higher-level military commands, and as a result conclude that "second echelon" depends upon the command level from which the enemy is viewed, the result is another of the numerous half-truths of conventional wisdom concerning the Soviets. For while "second echelon" forces do exist at a variety of levels, their existence is not merely a matter of perceptual perspective, but a Soviet organizational device that goes to the heart of their approach to command and control.[53]

The Soviet concept of echelonment defines the relationship between formations. The Soviet use of echelonment as a command and control device is generally misunderstood in the capitalist democracies. Echelonment is really a way of organizing for war. The Soviets apparently divide their armed forces into two strategic echelons: (1) forces more or less ready for war; and (2) forces mobilized for and generated during a conflict. Forces subordinated to a High Command in a theater of military action constitute the first strategic echelon. The first strategic echelon, representing organization for combat within a TMA, consists of fronts which constitute operational echelons that are internally echeloned. Echelonment within armies of an operational echelonment constitutes tactical echelonment. It is, therefore, theoretically possible to have a second echelon division (tactical echelon) of a second echelon army (operational echelon) of a second echelon front (also an operational echelon) of the first strategic echelon.

The Strategic Offensive

Current Soviet military art focuses in particular on the strategic offensive as the means of engaging and defeating the enemy. Using the combined operations of all services of the armed forces -- operating in land, air, and maritime areas -- Soviet forces are offense-oriented. Furthermore:

> The capabilities of strategic nuclear forces, with their enormous effective range, the increased striking power and maneuvering capabilities of the troops equipped with various types of combat vehicles, ensure the destruction of enemy armed forces units within the boundaries of the entire theater of military action and in its entire depth.[54]

The Soviet strategic offensive operation in a continental TMA would consist of several joint and combined-arms operations performed in accordance with a single concept and in conformity with a Supreme High Command plan for the defeat of an opponent in the theater. In a continental TMA, the major component operations of a strategic offensive, as defined by the Soviet military planners, may include the following types: air, anti-air, front, landing (air, amphibious, or joint), and naval. The strategic offensive also may include missile- and air-delivered nuclear strikes. Whether or not all or selective combinations of these operations are executed would depend on the actual battlefield environment, particularly on whether or not nuclear weapons were being used. The particular selection and subsequent repetition of the various operations would also be determined by the developing military and political situation.[55]

If the use of nuclear weapons in a strategic operation in a continental theater of military action is deemed necessary by the USSR, the armed forces would concentrate on targeting the enemy's nuclear delivery systems, nuclear storage areas, and airfields. The first or initial nuclear attack would be made with a large number of nuclear warheads delivered simultaneously or in quick succession against the entire target set. Regardless of how the Soviet Union chose to prosecute a conflict, however, it would still attempt to neutralize the enemy's air and nuclear assets and associated command, control, and communications (C^3) to the entire depth of the theater of military action. No matter what the weapons mix, the target set would remain the same.[56]

Ocean Operations

Soviet military documents have commented on naval operations in independent oceanic theaters of action:

> Strategic operations in oceanic theaters of action would be conducted to destroy enemy naval forces groups, its nuclear submarines, its large aircraft carrier task forces and countership forces, and also to foil enemy sea movements and to blockade islands and military naval bases. Such operations include the operations of one or more naval fleets, long-range aircraft and in some cases, the strikes of strategic nuclear forces and the actions of national air defense forces. Military actions expand in large areas of the ocean and assume a maneuvering, dynamic character.[57]

Airborne and amphibious assault are playing an increasingly important role in Soviet planning for deep operations within the context of theater warfare. On coastal axes, amphibious landings can assist in effecting envelopments. In addition to these activities in support of front offensive operations, landings may be undertaken as part of a naval operation. Airborne and amphibious assaults may also be directed against deep theater-strategic objectives as part of a strategic operation in a TMA.[58]

On maritime axes, operational-strategic landing operations would probably involve amphibious and airborne forces supported by naval surface combatants as well as aircraft of the navy and the air forces. In addition, such operations would be quickly reinforced by specially trained motorized rifle troops that would be airlanded or sealanded in the objective area. According to Soviet writers, the objectives of such operational-strategic airborne and/or amphibious operations include: (1) seizing important enemy administrative-political centers and industrial-economic regions; (2) disrupting enemy governmental and military control systems and centers; (3) seizing important maritime straits; (4) establishing a second front; and (5) forcing withdrawal from the war of selected governments of the enemy alliance.[59]

The naval operation in a strategic offensive operation in a continental TMA would include the destruction of opposing naval forces at sea, neutralization of opposing naval forces in their bases, and the defense of allied sea lines of communications in adjacent maritime areas, as well as the support of operations ashore. Such actions would fall under the immediate operational control of the High Command in the TMA.

Thus, strategic operations in oceanic or continental theaters of military action may be initiated and developed in different forms depending on the political and military situation. Should a war be "initiated with unlimited employment of nuclear weapons by the enemy, the strategic operation . . . starts with the initial nuclear strike."[60]   However, war may also be initiated and conducted without the use of nuclear weapons, although under the constant threat of nuclear attack.   "Under such circumstances, strategic operations can be initiated by air operations to destroy enemy air forces units and its nuclear weapons in the theater of military action."[61]   According to the Soviet General Staff, "the important condition to ensure success in such air operations is launching the initial strike in full surprise.   The enemy air forces should be attacked on their bases and its aircraft should be destroyed before they can fly."[62]

38

NOTES

1. Politicheskaya i voennaya geografiya (Political and military geography) Moskava: Voenizdat, 1980, pp. 92-93.
2. Ibid., p. 93.
3. Ibid.
4. S.N. Kozlov, The Officer's Handbook (Moscow: 1971, Washington: Government Printing Office, 1977). Soviet Military Thought, no. 13, published under the auspices of the United States Air Force, pp. 61-66.
5. Ibid, p. 65.
6. Ibid.
7. Ibid.
8. Lieutenant General P. Zhilin, "Uroki proshlogo i zaboty nastoyashchego" (Lessons of the past and concerns of the present), Kommunist (Communist), no. 7, May 1981, p. 73.
9. Ibid. As was noted by Soviet Chief of the General Staff Nikolay V. Ogarkov, "our armed forces will not simply defend themselves passively and wage purely defensive operations but will resolutely smash the aggressor." See "Ogarkov Article, Ceremony Mark Victory Day," Daily Report: Soviet Union, FBIS-SOV-82-097, 19 May 1982, Vol. III, no. 097, p. V5.
10. Lecture Materials from the Voroshilov General Staff Academy, "Strategic Operations In A Continental Theater of Military Operations."
11. Admiral Gorshkov, Naval Digest, no. 7, 1982.
12. Kozlov, The Officer's Handook, p. 58.
13. "Voyennaye iskusstovo" (Military art), Sovetskaya voyennaya entsikopedia (Soviet military encyclopedia -- hereafter, S.V.E.) Moskva: Voyenizdat, 1976, Vol. 7, p. 556.
14. Ibid.
15. Kozlov, The Officer's Handbook, p. 58.
16. "Strategiya voyennaya" (Military strategy), S.V.E., Moskva: Voyenizdat 1979, Vol. 7, p. 556.
17. Ibid., p. 564.
18. Ibid., p. 556.
19. "Operativnoye iskusstovo" (Operational art), Dictionary of Basic Military Terms (Moscow: 1965), Washington: Government Printing Office, p. 143.
20. Ibid.
21. "Voyennoye iskusstovo (Military art), S.V.E., p. 211.
22. Kozlov, p. 58. See also "Taktika (voyennaya)" (Military tactics), Dictionary of Basic Military Terms, p. 218.
23. "Voyennaya geografiya" (Military geography), Dictionary of Basic Military Terms, p. 37.
24. Lieutenant Commander (Dpl) Zygmunt Binieda, "Ogolne pojjecie teatru dzialan wojennych" (The general concept of a theater

of military action), Prezegladu morskiego (Polish Naval Review), no. 12, 1981, p. 3.

25. Ibid.

26. Politcheskaya i voyennaya geografiya (Political and military geography), Moskva: Voyenizdat, 1980, pp. 116-117.

27. Ibid.

28. "Teatr voiny" (Theater of war), S.V.E., Moskava: Voyenizdat, 1980, Vol. 8, p. 9.

29. Lecture Materials from the Voroshilov General Staff Academy, "General Concepts on Theaters of Military Action and Methods of Studying Their Strategic Characteristics."

30. Soviet Military Power, Washington: GPO, 1985, p. 12.

31. "Teatr voennykh deistvii (TVD)" (Theater of military action (TMA), Voennyi entsiklopedicheskii slovar (Military Encyclopedic Dictionary -- hereafter, V.E.S., Moskva: Voyenizdat, 1980, Vol. 8, p. 8.

32. "Teatr voyennykh deistvii" (Theater of military action), S.V.E., Moskva: Voyenizdat, 1980, Vol. 8, p. 8.

33. Great Soviet Encyclopedia, third edition, Vol. 25, 1976, p. 339.

34. "Podgotovka TVD," (Preparation of the TMA) S.V.E., Moscow: Voyenizdat, 1978, Vol. 6, p. 384.

35. Ogarkov, Always in Readiness to Defend the Homeland, p. 35.

36. Lecture Materials from the Voroshilow General Staff Academy, "General Concepts on Theaters of Military Action and Methods of Studying Their Strategic Characteristics."

37. Ibid; and "Teatr voyenny deistvii," S.V.E., pp. 8-9.

38. Partially compiled from the Lecture Materials from the Voroshilov General Staff Academy, "General Concepts on Theaters of Military Action and Methods of Studying their Strategic Characteristics" and "Classification of Theaters of Military Action."

39. Binieda, "The General Concept of a Theater of Military Action," p. 4.

40. "Strategicheskoe napravleniye" (Strategic Direction), S.V.E., Moscow: Voyenizdat, 1979, Vol. 7, p. 555; and, "Strategicheskoe napravleniye" (Strategic Direction), Dictionary of Basic Military Terms, p. 214.

41. Ibid.

42. "Operatsionnoye napravleniye" (Operational direction), Dictionary of Basic Military Terms, p. 145.

43. FM 100-2-3 (TBP FY 84), Soviet Army Troops Organization and Equipment, Coordinating Draft, August 1982, p. 1-10.

44. Ibid., pp. 1-10 and 1-11.

45. FM 100-2-1 (TBP FY 84), Soviet Army Operations and Tactics, Coordinating Draft, August 1982, pp. 4-2 and 4-3.

40

46. Colonel (Dipl) Pilot Aleksander Musial, "Character: zaczenie operacji powietrznych we wspolczenych dzialanizch wojennych" (The Character and Importance of Air Operations in Modern Warfare), Przeglad wojck lotniczych wojsk obrony powietrznej kraju (Polish Air Forces and Air Defense Review -- hereafter, Polish Air Review), no. 3, 1982.

47. Colonel-General P.K. Altukhov, editor, Osnovi teorii ypravleniya voiskami (The fundamentals of the theory of command and control), Moskva: Voyenizdat, 1984, p. 10.

48. Colonel M.P. Skirdo, The People, The Army, The Commander (Moscow: 1970), Washington: Government Printing Office, pp. 117 and 118.

49. I. Vyrodov, "Directing Operations of Strategic Troop Groups," Military-Historical Journal, no. 4, April 1979, JPRS, Translations of USSR Military Affairs, no. 1446, pp. 19-26.

50. Victor Suvorov, Inside the Army, New York: Macmillian Publishing Company, Inc., 1982, p. 41. This former GRU (Soviet military intelligence) officer defected in the late 1960s.

51. V. Kulikov, "Strategicheskoe rukovodstvo vooruzhennymi silami," Vizh., no. 6, June 1975, pp. 14 and 16.

52. Ogarkov, Always in Readiness to Defend the Homeland, pp. 34-35 and p. 60.

53. See "Glavnoe komandovanie" (High command), S.V.E., Vol. 2, Moskva: Voyenizdat, 1976, p. 562.

54. Lecture Materials from the Voroshilov General Staff Academy, "Strategic Operations In a Continental Theater of Military Action."

55. N.V. Ogarkov "Strategiya voyennaya" (Military Strategy), S.V.E., Moskva: Voyenizdat, 1978, 1978, Vol. 7, p. 564.

56. Major (Diploma) Wojciech Michalak, "Lotnictwo w dzialaniach rajdowo-manewrowych wojsk ladowych" (Aviation in Raid Maneuver Operations of Ground Forces), Przeglad wojck lotniczych woysk obrony powietrznej kraju (Polish Air Review, no. 2, 1982, p. 1.

57. Lecture Materials from the Voroshilov General Staff Academy, "Principles of Strategic Action of Armed Forces."

58. "Morskaya desantnaya operatsiya" (Naval landing operation), Voennyi-entsiklopedicheskii slovar (Military Encyclopedic Dictionary), Moskva: Voyenizdat, 1982, pp. 459-460; and "Vozdushno-desantnaya operatsiya" (Air-landing operation), V.E.S., p. 148.

59. "Desant" (Landing), SS.V.E., Vol. 3, 1977, pp. 152-156.

60. Lecture Materials from the Voroshilov General Staff Academy, "Strategic Operations In A Continental Theater of Military Action."

61. Ibid.

62. Ibid.

Chapter 4

POLITICAL DIMENSION OF SOVIET STRATEGY

Gerhard Wettig

The Soviet Concept of "Peaceful Coexistence"

Since 1956, any Soviet leadership has invariably subsumed its strategies toward the West under the label of "peaceful coexistence." That has, as is stressed in all relevant Soviet statements, a very important "meaning of principle" (printsipial'noe znachenie). Such characterization de-emphasizes the role of war in the direct East-West relationship. War between the two sides is seen as avoidable. Even more, on grounds of political principle the Kremlin feels that any outbreak of military hostilities with the United States and its allies should be avoided if possible. However, the postulate of "peaceful coexistence" presupposes a basic antagonism toward the West.

There may be "business-like relations" (delovye otnosheniia) where and when expedient, but such pragmatism cannot be accepted once matters of principle come into play. As soon as an issue is portrayed to be ideologically relevant, no approximation or understanding, not even a "truce," is allowed.

The antagonism inherent in the East-West relationship from the Soviet point of view has far-reaching implications. The "ideological struggle" (ideologicheskaia bor'ba) against the West may not be neglected. It is to take the forms both of challenging the international position of Western countries through political and military action in the Third World, and of exerting influence on the policies pursued by Western governments vis-a-vis the USSR through propaganda and mobilization campaigns.[1]

Even if East-West relations have reached a positive stage which the Soviet leaders hail as being consonant with the needs of "detente" (razriadka), the postulates of "ideological struggle" may not be de-emphasized. Since 1968, it is official Soviet doctrine that "ideological struggle" against the West necessarily intensifies when detente gains momentum.

Another implication of the inherent antagonism in the East-West relationship is the Soviet attitude on the problem of external security. In Moscow's view, prevention of war between East and West, while desirable, can nevertheless never be safely assured. For this reason, the USSR cannot base its security on war prevention, but must seek security through "successful defense," i.e., through a war-waging capability which will assure the enemy's defeat in case of war. The Soviet case-of-war security postulate does not allow the USSR to accept a mutual deterrence relationship with the North Atlantic Treaty Organization (NATO) and implies a superiority requirement for the Kremlin's armament effort.[2]

The maintenance of an antagonistic overall East-West relationship, on the one hand, and the Soviet need for a pragmatic business relationship with the West, on the other, are inherently contradictory elements of Soviet strategy toward West Europe. Frequently enough, the Soviet leadership is in favor of a relaxed, even cooperative relationship with a Western government, while at the same time it tries anything it can to mobilize domestic pressure against that same government,[3] and/or provides military support to forces which seek to break up Third World positions which are vital to the Western "partner."

In order to pursue such contradictory lines of policy, the Kremlin has conceptually divided international relations into two levels: "interstate relations" and "societal relations." When governments have to deal with governments, "business-like" intercourse seems appropriate. But as soon as the Communist Party of the Soviet Union (CPSU) and other East European communist parties enter into contact with societal forces in Western countries, and when they are trying to influence developments in third states outside the direct East-West relationship, the principle of antagonism against the political order represented by Western governments has to be accorded priority.

The restraints of peacefulness inherent in the Soviet peaceful coexistence doctrine therefore apply only to those aspects of East-West relations which concern direct government-to-government and direct state-to-state interaction, i.e., the behavior to be observed by the government leaders and both the civil-diplomatic services and the military forces when they are directly dealing with one another. In any other respect, a more antagonistic kind of relationship is pursued by Soviet leaders which, to be sure, is calculated to provide the USSR with unilaterally favorable opportunities for political influence.

As the late Soviet leader and CPSU theroetician Mikhail Suslov put it, the "ideological struggle" between the two camps is to be waged both between the societies of East and West and within the societies of Western countries, but it should not be allowed to take place in Eastern societies.[4] Almost four decades of Soviet policies have amply made plain that the West Europe area has always been the prime focus of Moscow's attempts to exert influence on the West at the societal level. No other Western region is as easily accessible to the Soviet leaders nor offers greater prospects for an impact on world affairs.

Basic Soviet Goals in West Europe

In a general sense, Soviet strategy toward West Europe has been based on Moscow's unwillingness to accept either a West Europe under an American-Atlantic aegis (i.e., the North Atlantic Treaty Organization) or an independent West European entity which would combine its resources (as was advocated by French President Charles de Gaulle). Moscow has carefully avoided being confronted with the choice between these two possibilities, so that not even a relative preference for one or the other alternative as a "lesser evil" can be inferred.[5]

Soviet refusal to accept either West European political-military arrangement can mean but one thing: The leaders in Moscow regard the whole of Europe as their "natural" political domain and for this reason want West Europe to forego any option of power/political independence vis-a-vis the USSR if and when the United States pulls out.

Moscow thus seeks hegemony over a West Europe consisting of separated nations. If the cohesion of NATO had been severely damaged by West European or West German unwillingness to honor the alliance's dual-track Intermediate Range Nuclear Forces (INF) deployment decision of December 12, 1979, such a prospect might not have been totally unrealistic.

The Soviet leaders do not think it wise to make public their aims for hegemony over West Europe. Nevertheless, Vadim Zagladin, the first deputy of the CPSU's Central Committee Department on International Relations with specific responsibility for West European affairs, made his view plain to two West German journalists who had asked him whether he felt that the West Europeans should seek neutrality (i.e., opt themselves out of NATO). He said, "That would be unrealistic in the short run, although we have always stood for a dissolution of the blocs and still have that in mind as a long-term goal."[6]

The attainment of that goal would not mean that the West Europeans have to go communist, but it would imply that their foreign and security policies would have to be made under the shadow of Soviet power. The West European countries would have to seek agreement with the USSR in all issues regarded as vital by Moscow and thus have to adapt themselves to external conditions created by Moscow.

West Germany in Soviet Strategy Toward West Europe

The Soviet leaders act on the assumption that the Federal Republic of Germany (FRG) is the crucial factor in West Europe. In their view, neither NATO nor the European Community could work without the West Germans. De Gaulle's decision of 1966 to leave the Military Organization of NATO largely contributed to the importance of the FRG in NATO. Once France was no longer militarily available to NATO, only the FRG continued to provide the Atlantic Alliance with both the territory and the forces necessary for putting up a defense on the European continent. Also, there are no other garrisons imaginable for the American troops which the West Europeans regard as an indispensable element of their security. It follows for Moscow that no NATO country on the European continent would be willing to place confidence in the alliance if the FRG no longer participates.[7] The Soviet judgment that it is West Germany's attitude which counts most in West Europe has been reconfirmed during the missile deployment controversy.[8]

Moscow has used both carrots and sticks in attempts to make the West Germans give up their commitment to NATO. Soviet behavior during 1966 provided telling examples. First, the leaders of the Soviet Union made an abortive attempt to lure the Social Democratic Party (SPD) into an "all-German" commonality with the East German communists in the hope of providing an "all-German" dynamism in the Eastern direction.

At the end of the year, the formation of a "big coalition" government in Bonn based on both Christian Democratic Union/Christian Socialist Union (CDU/CSU) and SPD made the Soviet leaders feel that Gaullist tendencies were on the rise in West German politics and should find encouragement and support from Moscow. It was only after that expectation had proved wrong that the Kremlin finally decided to accuse the FRG of incurable "revanchism" and "militarism," which were said to put Europe's peace and security into jeopardy. From then on, a Soviet strategy designed to place maximum pressure on West Germany from both inside and outside the country, has been applied in an effort to wear down its pro-NATO stand.[9]

Different tactics for the same purpose have been used in the early 1980s. Chancellor Helmut Schmidt's SPD-FDP (Free Democratic Party) government was courted in Moscow for its willingness to conduct business with the USSR and its allies at a time when Washington had responded to Soviet military intervention in Afghanistan with economic sanctions. This cooperative behavior paid handsomely as both the Soviet Union and its East European allies profited economically.

Furthermore, a serious political rift between the FRG and the United States began to open. Also, an increasing part of the West

German public became convinced that the country could relieve its detente relationship with the Warsaw Pact states from the alleged burden of what was called U.S. unreasonableness, if only Bonn stuck to the "dialogue" with Moscow.

However, the Soviet side took great pains to mobilize the West Germans against Schmidt's government and to create public pressure against honoring the missile deployment pledge to NATO. At the same time, the Kremlin leaders frustrated the chancellor's sustained efforts to reach a mutually acceptable diplomatic compromise on the missiles. Such a deal would have made a decisive contribution to the domestic stabilization of the SPD-led West German government, as it would have solved some basic dilemmas with which the chancellor was confronted in his own political party. The Soviet leaders were quite aware of their potential for help, but they deliberately chose a course which was bound to make Schmidt's downfall ever more likely -- obviously in the confident belief that the West German domestic scene subsequently would become more pacifist and neutralist. These hopes, however, have proven to be illusory. In the end Moscow's dual strategy toward Schmidt's government failed to produce the desired anti-NATO outcome.

The Decoupling Strategy

The persistent Soviet effort to break the FRG out of the Western deployment consensus and, thereby, to keep the American INF missiles out of Europe altogether, has to be seen as part of a wider political design. The Soviet postulate of security implies, as has already been noted, the requirement of military superiority. This applies particularly to the European theater. Soviet statements on the correlation of military forces indicate that the Soviet leaders are sufficiently confident that they can muster superior military strength there. But so far, they find it problematical to put their European military advantage to practical use, as U.S. policies of extending the mutual deterrence relationship between the two superpowers to Europe invalidate whatever potential for victory and pressure the USSR may possess.

Thus Moscow is being prevented from exploiting its claim to military superiority vis-a-vis the West Europeans, as it has to take into account that a conflict in Europe is under some risk of eventually escalating to a global-strategic exchange between the United States and the USSR. Such a risk, even if it were only a relatively small one, is one that the Soviet leadership is definitely not willing to take.

The present situation imposes restrictions on Soviet strategy toward West Europe. Whenever there is a prospect of acute tensions, Kremlin leaders have to be cautious. The same goes for the Western countries. The Kremlin cannot afford the risk of war, and has to display political restraint accordingly. This state of affairs, however, is dissonant with what is regarded as a basic security need in Moscow. The Soviet view presupposes that the danger of war between East and West cannot be eliminated and accordingly requires that the challenge of potential warfare must be met by a usable war-waging capability. The unavailability of such a capability is bound to be perceived as a grave security deficit. How can the USSR be secure if it cannot stand the crucial test of a war which after all must be faced as an enduring real possibility? The problem is seen to be particularly relevant with regard to the European theater, as that theater constitutes the primary field of East-West conflict.

What prevents the Soviet Union from making its superior military theater capability felt in Europe is the U.S. global-strategic deterrent which has been extended from the direct superpower relationship to the European theater by means of "coupling." The United States has declared that it will stand for its European allies' security in much the same way as it stands for the security of its own territory, and it has reinforced that statement by warning the USSR that any deadly threat to the allies' security might trigger an escalatory process which might end up with a global-strategic duel.

The message to Moscow is that it cannot exploit any available military advantage against the U.S. European allies without incurring the risks which are inherent in the bilateral deterrence relationship of the superpowers. In Soviet eyes, the restraint imposed on the USSR by Washington must be accepted as long as there is a credible U.S. capacity to escalate. Therefore, Soviet efforts to get rid of the restraint which makes the USSR's superior military theater capability in Europe unusable concentrate primarily on U.S. means of escalation designed for coupling.

The Soviet leadership is conscious of Washington's unwillingness to allow itself to be confronted with an all-or-nothing choice. That is to say, the Kremlin realizes that the United States is determined both to break the deterrent threat of escalation into selective steps and to put the onus of the escalatory choice on the USSR. Washington will not threaten escalation directly to the global-strategic level.[10] The Soviet leadership views this as an opportunity to be exploited.

If the United States can be denied the necessary intermediate escalatory capabilities and if it can be deprived not only of escalation dominance, but also of any minimum capacity to escalate in the European theater, Washington may well be persuaded that it has no longer an option of escalation and that it therefore cannot possibly continue its coupling policies. After several successive U.S. governments had refused to make a deal with the USSR on decoupling,[11] the Kremlin leaders have concentrated on the attempt to render the American INF capabilities inefficient and to establish Soviet escalation dominance in Europe. Consequently, they have regarded a Soviet monopoly in modern INF systems vis-a-vis the United States as indispensible.[12]

If the Soviet leaders had succeeded in their decoupling effort, the implications would have been far-reaching. Within a foreseeable future, the USSR would have achieved a unilateral war-making capability in Europe. This is not to say that Moscow would be willing to go to war from then on. Rather the political correlation of forces would have changed fundamentally. The Soviet leaders would find it easy to declare vital interests to be at stake, whenever disagreement of some substance with West Europe should arise, and would thus find it easy to impress the other side with the prospect of acute tension and crisis.

If the West Europeans decided that they could not afford war, they would be subject to pressure to resolve the political conflict by adapting themselves to Soviet desires. That in turn would increasingly convince them of NATO's inability to provide protection, with the likely eventual outcome being the collapse of the North Atlantic Alliance and a U.S. withdrawal.

This scenario involving the Soviet decoupling strategy has much explanatory power for the purposes of analysis. It provides a plausible explanation of why the issue of deployment or non-deployment, and of coupling or decoupling, has been so much at the center of Soviet strategy toward West Europe. It also makes clear that Moscow's desire (which has been given expression by Zagladin) to make the West Europeans opt out of NATO is not declaratory in nature, but constitutes operational policy.

The Kremlin's offensive political strategy is closely interrelated with what tends to be regarded as an exclusively defensive strategic objective: security. It is through military superiority[13] plus decoupling from the U.S.-USSR deterrence relationship that the Soviet leaders seek the case-of-war security which they feel is necessary in the European theater. This combination also provides for Soviet political victory over its Western rivals. In Moscow's view, this is the political corollary of military security: to safeguard the Soviet sphere's immunity from all kinds of undesirable foreign influence at both the "interstate" and the "societal" levels, by extending Soviet control to the sources of such undesirable foreign influence.

The psychological need for this is created by the peculiarities of the Soviet system. All political mechanisms are based on the assumption that order must be maintained through central control over almost any aspect of life. Any influence which defies the regime's control is viewed as a threat to the regime's functioning.[14] The security needs which the Soviet leaders perceive in relation to the outside world tend to be unlimited and to expand ever further.

Wherever and whenever the correlation of forces (which is given decisive political importance in Soviet thinking) has provided a low-risk opportunity for satisfying such security needs, the Soviet leaders have acted accordingly. Countries which want to guard their independence cannot allow Moscow to have a free ride concerning their security needs. Instead, the principle of equal security to all countries, whether big or small, should apply. That means in practice that no power, including the USSR, should be allowed a war-making capability. This insures a mutually compelling interest in war prevention and consequently a mutually respected immunity from war threat and coercive pressure.

Soviet Appeals for "Military Detente"

The Soviet decoupling strategy is complemented by efforts designed to promote "military detente" in Europe. The meaning of that term has never been explained by the USSR, but it can be inferred from the functional context in which the term has been employed. The basic Soviet argument is that the NATO countries are under no necessity to arm. They allegedly need not defend themselves because the USSR is a peaceful power and does not threaten anyone. Whoever in the West ascribes a threat potential to the Soviet Union does so for purposes of his own. The logic of the argument leads to the Soviet conclusion that any increases in West European military capabilities are indicative of aggressive intent.

The message which the Kremlin tries to convey when it talks about the need for "military detente" in Europe is that the West countries can, indeed should, disarm so as not to be confronted with the charge of aggressiveness. It goes without saying that the USSR and its allies are not judged by the same standard. Regardless of whether NATO's defense efforts increase or decrease, Moscow has always asserted that the socialist states have to defend themselves against a military challenge which is increasing all the time.[15]

Soviet policies of "military detente" have included support for renunciation of force treaties; calls for a permanent all-European body to safeguard security and peace in the region; denuclearization proposals, e.g., the creation of nuclear-free zones, which would apply to European countries outside the USSR; and, efforts to achieve agreement on no first-use of nuclear weapons.

The Substitute for Arms Control

Another aspect of Moscow's strategy toward Western Europe has been the effort to frame Western arms reduction proposals to justify Soviet claims to a say in West European defense policies.

Moscow has sought to exploit the Mutual Balanced Force Reduction (MBFR) negotiations for that purpose. The MBFR proposals tabled by the USSR were designed to pinpoint the force structures of Central Europe in much detail. On such a basis, the Soviet leadership could have persuasively argued that not only numerical ceilings, but also structural patterns of NATO's forces in Central Europe, had been agreed upon which could be changed only with Soviet consent. In this case, the area of military reductions under MBFR was bound to become an area of military control by the out-of-area participants of the MBFR agreement.

The Soviet leadership also attempted to redirect Western proposals when the NATO and "neutral and nonaligned" participants of the Conference for Security and Cooperation in Europe (CSCE) pressed for what was called "confidence-building measures in the military domain." The idea underlying the quest for such confidence-building measures is that mutual agreement on measures providing for transparency and predictability in each other's military behavior should increasingly eliminate existing opportunities for war initiatives without the opponent receiving timely warning.

Those who recommend these measures feel that if one removes the likelihood of military surprise, one removes a crucial cause of insecurity and creates a more stable relationship. The Soviet leaders have never espoused that philosophy. On the contrary, they have held that it would be to the West's unilateral advantage if confidence-building measures were adopted, as it is NATO, not the Warsaw Pact, which holds options of attack and surprise in Europe. Therefore, the Soviet negotiators at the CSCE, at the follow-up meetings, and at the Conference on Confidence-Building Measures and Disarmament in Europe (CDE) accepted only token changes.

At the same time, however, the Kremlin has sought to exploit the confidence-building measures issue for its own purposes. The Western, neutral, and non-aligned interest in military confidence-building could provide a starting point for the establishment of a special zone west of the Soviet borders which might gradually turn into an arms control zone susceptible to a Soviet <u>droit</u> <u>de</u> <u>regard</u>.[16]

Accordingly, the Soviet negotiators at the CSCE have fiercely tried to have the USSR's territory left out, and have conceded only that a small border strip could be included. That Moscow's representatives at the Madrid CSCE follow-up meeting finally acquiesced to a mandate for the CDE which envisaged discussion on confidence-building measures for all of Europe including the USSR up to the Urals was due to the Soviet leaders' sensing a particularly strong need for the CDE to get started at the time.

When the CDE had finally begun, the Soviet delegation did not feel prevented from ignoring the topic agreed upon and demanded declaratory security arrangements instead. It also made an express attempt to exempt the USSR from prospective agreements on military matters.

Soviet zeal to establish nuclear-free zones in the rest of Europe is also a telling case. Among other things, such an arrangement would imply that the USSR (which would assure the nuclear-free countries of their not being exposed to nuclear attack in return for their willingness not to tolerate any nuclear weapon on their soil) must be given the possibility to make sure always whether the nuclear-free countries are really living up to their contractual promise. This could provide a suitable basis for Soviet supervision of all defense-related potentials and activities in the area. In Moscow's proposals for a nuclear-free zone in Scandanavia, such an intent has already clearly surfaced.[17]

To sum up, in its strategy toward West Europe, the Soviet leadership tries to put all kinds of arms control, force reduction and other security-related schemes to use for the following purposes:

o   To have the European territory west of its borders, i.e., basically the European countries outside the Warsaw Pact, thinned out militarily. This is in order to confirm and intensify Soviet theater superiority.

o   To take military and political options, most notably deterrence-through-escalation, self-determined defense structuring, and West European pooling of resources, away from NATO. This would enlarge the scope of feasible Soviet action vis-a-vis the West.

o   To change West Europe's power structures both internally and relative to the USSR. This would subject the countries outside the Soviet orbit increasingly to Moscow's claim to a say in West European affairs.

Concluding Comments

One of the principal tasks assigned to Soviet propaganda is to prevent the West European public from forming adequate perceptions of what goals Moscow pursues and what methods it employs. The Soviet Union is portrayed as the offended party in the East-West relationship. Also, key notions like "superiority," "equilibrium," or "offensive military strategy" are given hidden meanings different from common usage so that the public in the West cannot gauge what Soviet statements really mean.[18]

We have referred to the dual "interstate" and "societal" character of Soviet strategy which in turn produces a close coordination of efforts in the fields of diplomacy and of public information strategy. As the dual character of the Kremlin's West European strategy has been neglected in Western analyses, and therefore has not been taken into due account by Western policymakers, the crucial problem of how diplomatic and public information actions are synchronized in Moscow also has not been addressed. It urgently needs investigation if Soviet strategy is to be more fully understood and effectively responded to.

That leading Western politicians have been unaware of the "societal" level of Soviet global strategy, and of the political possibilities it accords to the Kremlin, has become most obvious in the case of the dual-track decision. The political calculus of its authors was based on the assumption that they could confront the Soviet leadership with a choice between either accepting a mutually satisfactory INF limitation agreement or having to face Western counterdeployment. It was judged that the leading people in Moscow saw counterdeployment as the greater evil (which may well have been correct) and that therefore they could not but acquiesce in a negotiated solution tolerable to NATO (which was utterly wrong). This fundamental assessment prevented the leading Western statesmen from realizing that the Soviet leadership felt it had a good chance to avoid counterdeployment without having to accept INF limitations on itself, as it had various means and ways by which it could exert or promote intense domestic pressure on several West European governments, particularly on the government in Bonn.

The major goal of Soviet political strategy toward West Europe at present is to undermine NATO and to push the United States out of Europe -- without even the slightest indication of a concomitant willingness to ease Soviet control over East Europe. Achievement of this goal would give the USSR its "natural" hegemonial role on the whole continent.[19] But this anti-NATO goal of Moscow cannot be reconciled with the vital political interests of the Western countries on both sides of the Atlantic. On that basis, there is certainly no prospect for East-West agreement.

Moscow's intent, if to be taken into due account and to be responded to adequately by the North Atlantic Alliance, is not the only factor which determines the course of the East-West conflict and hence the possibilities for potential agreement between the two sides. What the Soviet leaders want to achieve cannot be realized simply because of its being desired. Other conditions also have to be met.

Western policies will determine whether Soviet strategies can be successfully implemented as well as whether Soviet goals can be finally achieved. If the leaders of the West perceive the challenge correctly and find ways and means to respond accordingly, the efforts by the Kremlin are bound to be frustrated. If the Soviet leadership is denied superiority and decoupling and has to accept a relationship of equilibrium in Europe, this will sooner or later be

52

reflected in Soviet negotiating behavior. The Kremlin has far-reaching ambitions, it is true, but its policies are nonetheless adapted to practical realities. For example, it rejects mutual deterrence and opts for war-fighting capability on grounds of principle, but it respects mutual deterrence as a fact when it is there. Indeed the cognitive patterns of Soviet ideology imply that the highest priority be given to due recognition of existing realities, even if those realities clearly run counter to expressed desires.

The strongly emphasized dependence of Soviet decision-making on reckoning with what is real gives Soviet strategy a distinctly opportunistic note. The calculus of the chances and risks involved in potential future actions largely determines which course is being regarded as feasible. Therefore, there is no such thing as a detailed "master plan" or strategy guiding Soviet international actions. Rather, in Moscow's flexible strategy toward West Europe, the world opportunities both foreseen and unforeseen are exploited when they arise, while actions deemed desirable on grounds of principle are not taken if they seem to entail serious risk.[20]

That does not mean that the impact of Soviet intent should be seen as negligible. Such intent certainly provides for strong preference in both positive and negative respects. But the leaders in Moscow follow their preferences only as far as they feel they can afford on the basis of existing realities. If they can be persuaded over an extended period that their attempts to act on this or that preference are utterly futile, they will finally shelve their desires for the time being and accept another basis for East-West interaction. This then could provide a basis for agreement on issues which had looked unsolvable before.

53

NOTES

1. The Soviet attempt not to allow NATO's dual-track decision of December 12, 1979, to be implemented by fostering the anti-deployment movement in West European countries is a very telling example. For the Kremlin's relevant action, see Gerhard Wettig, "The Western Peace Movement in Moscow's Longer View," Strategic Review, Vol. XII, no. 2 (Spring 1984), pp. 44-54.

2. For comments on and Soviet documents on these important points, see the notes accompanying Wettig's original paper.

3. A case in point is Soviet behavior toward the West German government of Helmut Schmidt in 1980-1982.

4. Address by Mikhail Suslov, 13 July, Pravda, 14 July 1973.

5. See Eberhard Schulz, Moskau und die europaische Integration (Munich-Vienna: R. Oldenbourg, 1975); and, Gerhard Wettig, Community and Conflict in the Socialist Camp (New York: St. Martin's, 1975).

6. "Spiegel" interview with Vadim Zagladin, Der Spiegel, June 8, 1981, p. 119.

7. See, e.g., Opasnye tendentsii, in: Novoe vremia, 6/1967, p. 4; V. Kriukov, Germanskii vopros i sovremennost', in: Mezhdunarodnaia zhizn', 2/1967, p. 19; V intersekh prochnogo mira, in: Mezhdunarodnaia zhizn', 6/1967, pp. 5-6.

8. Cf. V. Saposhnikov, O nekotorykh problemkh sovremennogo antivoennogo dvizheniia, in: Mirovaia ekonomika i mezhdunarodnye otnosheniia, 12/1981, p. 23.

9. See Wettig, Community and Conflict in the Socialist Camp, pp. 20-32.

10. For the U.S. concept, see the explanation by an author of Presidential Directive 59: Walter Slocombe, "The Countervailing Strategy," International Security, Vol. 4, Spring 1981, pp. 18-27.

11. The Soviet decoupling effort has been evident ever since Soviet diplomacy began demanding the elimination of the U.S. "forward-based systems" in the SALT I context. The most striking example was Gromyko's and Brezhnev's proposal to Kissinger in September 1972 that the two superpowers secretly agree on not allowing a conventional and/or tactical-nuclear East-West war in Europe to affect each other's territory. Henry Kissinger, Years of Upheaval (London: Weidenfeld & Nicholson, 1982), pp. 236-239.

12. During the INF negotiations in Geneva, the Soviet side had one objective: to preserve its massive SS-20 and "BACKFIRE" arsenal with little or no reduction and to avoid any PERSHING II or cruise missile deployment. See, Progress Report on Intermediate-Range Nuclear Forces to Ministers by the Special Consultative Group, December 8, 1983, NATO Information Service, Brussels; Gerhard Wettig, "How the INF Negotiations in Geneva Failed," Aussenpolitik. German Foreign Affairs Review, 2/1984, pp. 123-139.

That objective was unanimously stated by the chief Soviet negotiator, when the INF talks began (see John Barry, "Geneva Behind Closed Doors," The Times, May 31, 1983).

13. Cf. Harry Gelman, The Brezhnev Politburo and the Decline of Detente (Ithaca, NY: Cornell University Press, 1984), pp. 38-42.

14. Cf. Peter Robejsek, "Zur Frage der Expansivitat in der sowjetischen Aubenpolitik, Ursachen und Antriebskrafte," in Osteuropa, 4/1984, pp. 265-274.

15. The discrepancy between the alleged and the real armament of NATO was particularly noticable during the first half of the 1970s when most Western countries including the United States decreased their defense expenditures, while Soviet propaganda decried a huge Western arms buildup. At the same time, the USSR had a continuous annual military budget increase of 4-5 percent, according to Western estimates.

16. Cf. B.N. Ponomarev, O roli uchenykh v ukreplenii mezhdunarodnoi bezopasnosti, in: Vestnik Akademii Nauk SSSR, 9/1983, p. 16; Johan Jorgen Holst, Abshreckung und Stabilitat im Verhaltnis zwischen NATO und Warschauer Pakt, in: Europz-Archiv, 1/1981, pp. 11-12, 16; Gerhard Wettig, Sicherheitspolitische Vertrauensbildung in den Ost-West-Beziehungen, in: Friedens-Warte, 1-4/1980, pp. 49-67.

17. See Robert K. German, "Nuclear-Free Zones: Norwegian Interest, Soviet Encouragement," Orbis, Vol. 26, no. 2, Summer 1982, p. 453.

18. This point has been more fully elaborated by the author in: Krafteverhaltnis, Kriegsverhutung und Kriegfuhrung in sowjetischer Darstellung, Berichte des Bundesinstituts fur ostwissenschaftliche und internationale Studien, Nr. 42/1983, pp. 27-40.

19. For a similar evaluation on the basis of other evidence see John Van Oudenaren, "The Soviet Union and Eastern Europe: Options for the 1980s and Beyond," Santa Monica/CA: The Rand Corporation (R-3136-AF), March 1984, pp. 13-17, 74-78.

20. See also loc. cit., p. 12.

Chapter 5

ECONOMIC DIMENSION OF SOVIET STRATEGY

Giuseppe Schiavone

The Kremlin and the Soviet Economy

Nowadays, the poor performance of the Soviet economy and the marked decline in ideological dynamism, labor discipline, and civic morale, which are denounced by the Soviet press and official party documents, appear to be scarcely conducive to the realization of the USSR's long-range goal of "catching up and overtaking" the West. This goal, in fact, was enshrined in the Communist Party program which was drawn up in 1961 during the Khrushchev period.[1] In 1984, Chernenko, General Secretary of the Communist Party of the Soviet Union (CPSU), urged the commission charged with the revision of the program for consideration by the 27th CPSU Congress in 1986 to take a more realistic view on the present condition and future prospects of the capitalist system whose "reverses of development" are far from being exhausted.[2]

In all likelihood, the Soviet leadership now faces a much less felicitous political and socio-economic situation, at home and abroad, than that which prevailed during the Brezhnev era.[3] If a sustained improvement in Soviet-American relations fails to materialize, it may prove to be a hard task for the Kremlin leaders to match what is desirable in terms of the long-standing goal of increasing the USSR's share of world power and what is attainable in terms of the constraints of arms racing and the requirement of crucial domestic economic and anticorruption reforms.

It would probably be naive to believe that purely economic and financial concerns can substantially enhance the attractiveness to the Kremlin of a return, albeit temporary, to detente. However, it may be argued that detente appears as a significant complement to the attempts at easing domestic economic problems. Although a return to detente should not necessarily involve a historic shift in Soviet policy, it would doubtless effect a major change in strategy with largely unforeseeable consequences.

As a matter of fact, besides the well-known themes of conventional Soviet discourse on foreign policy and strategy, concepts of global economic and technological interdependence have been introduced in Soviet theory and practice since the early 1970s, at the heyday of detente. In the period immediately following the 24th CPSU Congress of 1971, General Secretary Brezhnev, Prime Minister Kosygin and other Soviet leaders repeatedly emphasized the need to expand economic ties with the "capitalist" countries. The growing commitment to purchases of Western machinery, equipment, and foodstuffs was presented as essential not only to the development of the domestic economy -- ensuring the benefits of international industrial specialization and transfer of technology -- but also to broader participation of the USSR in international economic affairs.

Unambiguous evidence of strong pressures to reform Soviet foreign economic policy and strategy emerged at the Plenum of the CPSU Central Committee in April 1973, with the decision of significantly extending trade and economic relations with the outside world, notably the Western countries.[4] It may be interesting to note that the new approach to international economic relations materialized on a larger scale in 1974 when the 28th Session of the Council for Mutual Economic Assistance (CMEA) amended the organization's charter with a view, inter alia, to broadening the scope of activities on the international level. The session viewed with favor the possible establishment of formal ties with the European Economic Community (EEC) as well as the expansion of economic relations with non-member countries, irrespective of their social and political systems.[5]

The Soviet scheme for developing wide-ranging economic cooperation with the West soon met with both domestic opposition and outside impediments. Suffice it to mention, among the latter, the adoption by the U.S. Congress of the Jackson-Vanik and Stevenson amendments which respectively denied the USSR most-favored-nation treatment -- by establishing a linkage, wholly unacceptable in Moscow's view, between the concession of such treatment by the United States and the emigration policies of the recipient country -- and severely limited cheap government credits. The sharp deterioration in the international political environment in the late 1970s and early 1980s inevitably brought about a retreat from detente, to the detriment of East-West economic cooperation.

U.S. sanctions concerning trade and technology, adopted as a response to Soviet direct and/or indirect intervention in sensitive areas of the Third World and to the imposition of martial law in Poland, gave rise in the USSR to hostility for any major expansion of Soviet reliance on economic and technological ties with the West.

Despite warnings against allegedly unnecessary imports of foreign technology and goods, which could be substituted by domestic production, top Soviet officials and experts have been stressing, over the past few years, the need for continued international, and especially East-West, economic, scientific, and technological cooperation, thereby rejecting autarky as a viable alternative. Soviet-Western cooperation is described "as a process for deepening the international division of labor and accelerating scientific and technological progress which in its turn increases mutual interest in economic cooperation between countries with differing social and economic systems."[6]

As a matter of fact, increased East-West trade and cooperation may ultimately prove, in Soviet eyes, to provide a far safer path -- both politically and economically -- to overcoming the USSR's most pressing economic problems than the introduction of a large-scale change in a system which has remained virtually unmodified since the five-year plans were originally brought into use in the late 1920s.[7] On the other hand, no far-reaching economic reform could be successfully undertaken without a marked improvement in the international environment -- be it detente or something else -- and a limitation of military expenditures.

Given the hard and painful choices which the Kremlin leadership faces in the current decade, it may be argued that economic constraints will play a major role in shaping foreign policy in general and foreign economic policy in particular. Although no collapse in the domestic economy is to be expected, the declining growth rates of both industrial and agricultural output as well as an unprecedented situation of resource stringency place a heavy strain on the Soviet system as a whole. In the years since World War II, Soviet economic growth has been characterized by constantly diminishing rates.

According to CIA estimates, Soviet GNP rose at 5.3 percent a year in 1966-70, at 3.8 percent in 1971-75, and then at only 2.7 percent in 1976-80. Growth rates stood at 1.8 percent in 1981 and 2.0 percent in 1982. An increase in the growth rate occurred in 1983 and continued in the first half of 1984. Nonetheless, several analysts believe that in the 1980s the annual rate of growth will at best be in the 2 to 2.5 percent range while the risk of virtual stagnation cannot be ruled out altogether.

The various Soviet elites involved in the policymaking process seem well aware of the economy's bottlenecks and of the troubles in several key industries; in several official statements ever since the last years of the Brezhnev era the necessity for changes in planning, management, and economic mechanisms has been openly acknowledged. Articles in the Soviet press,[8] as well as academic works, [9] have provided a wealth of arguments to both supporters and opponents of major changes in the economic system. At present no thorough economic reform appears to be in the making, while the results of the labor discipline campaign initiated under Andropov and of other recent measures are far from impressive. The compromise embodied in the Eleventh Five-Year Plan (1981-1985) and apparently based on a deliberate slowdown of investment growth with a view to ensuring growth of military expenditures and consumption, has not worked in practice.[10]

To avoid a further slowdown from past performance, planners and policymakers must assess the complex trade-offs between the competing claims of investment, consumption, and defense spending. The last-named item is naturally connected with the international role of the USSR -- a role that is ultimately decided not by the Kremlin alone but depends on the relative strengths and weaknesses of the USSR's potential adversaries.

It is a moot point whether the present Soviet leadership, which is undergoing the replacement of many of its aging and ailing members within a relatively brief time, will be bold enough to undertake the task of effecting a far-reaching economic reform. The apparent recovery of 1983 and the first half of 1984 seems to have relieved the pressures for large-scale changes, at least for the time being. The military establishment will doubtless play a very significant role in influencing the party's decisions on this central issue in Soviet affairs, either delaying or expediting the task of institutional change.

However Soviet civilian and military leaders assess the performance of the economic system and its development prospects in the middle and late 1980s, it is increasingly apparent that a cut in defense spending may become necessary within the next few years if present standards of living are to be preserved.

Consumption in general has been under pressure since the early 1980s and the risk of widespread popular discontent is too serious a matter to be taken lightly by Soviet authorities. Presumably the military are coming to realize that defense is unlikely to resume in the foreseeable future its earlier growth rates and may no longer be viewed as the priority of priorities. The day may still be far off when Soviet leaders begin to abandon the traditional siege mentality, but harsh economic reality at home and the pressing necessity for international cooperation -- especially with the West -- should make a return to detente not implausible.

Soviet-East European Economic Relations in a Time of Change

East Europe, no longer a stable and viable element of the Soviet system, has come under increasing challenge, not from without but from within. The case for far-reaching economic reform is stressed throughout the region where the patent inability of the system of central planning to promote "intensive" growth, through more efficient use of labor and capital and improved technical competence, is a cause of considerable concern.[11] As a matter of fact, greater reliance on efficiency and technological innovation has proved insufficient when it is not accompanied by structural change in the centralized economic systems.

The broad guidelines established by the 1984 CMEA summit meeting will contribute to shaping the next set of five-year plans (1986-90), but growth prospects of the East European countries will also depend on a variety of internal and external factors, including the state of Western economies and their trade and credit policies. According to a number of Western analysts, however, East Europe's economic exposure vis-a-vis the West is likely to decline for the rest of the 1980s, while dependence on the USSR will be growing. Though signs of recovery from recession became evident in the first half of 1984, it need not be stressed that the current pace of growth in East Europe remains well below the postwar trend; on the whole, many countries of the region should find it very difficult to abide by key commitments of their economic plans.

Nearly all East European countries, which had borrowed heavily on Western capital markets in the 1970s and had to service increased debt obligations, have succeeded to a remarkable extent in obtaining current account surpluses and reducing their net hard-currency debt by boosting exports vigorously and restraining imports.[12] The overall improvement in the region's hard-currency position has not occurred without substantial cost. Many analysts are convinced that sharp cutbacks in investments over the past few years will adversely affect growth prospects and living standards in East Europe for the rest of the decade. Furthermore, it is not unlikely that poor economic performance will translate into political unrest and social instability. In fact, economic viability is generally viewed as an essential element of political stability in East Europe.

The special relationship with the USSR gives rise to substantial constraints on domestic policies in East Europe, especially as regards the possible linkage between economic reform and political liberalization. However, the reform measures adopted so far have avoided the real issues of development strategy and genuine structural change which might generate pressures for similar innovations in the political system. As a matter of fact, any East European policymaker planning to introduce far-reaching changes must carefully take into account not only the costs, both economic and political, of noncompliance with Soviet demands and expectations but also the possible reactions by other countries of the region which may be affected by such changes.[13]

Whatever the extent and efficacy of East European efforts to deal with problems which stem from built-in systemic weaknesses, the economic choices and constraints facing the Soviet leadership in East Europe have undergone a substantial change. The USSR's outright economic exploitation of East European countries, which was a salient characteristic of the early postwar years, has gradually changed into a situation of large-scale economic assistance (direct and indirect) extended by the USSR to its East European partners.

Over the past decade, large "implicit" subsidies have been provided by the USSR, mainly in the form of concessionary pricing, especially for energy and non-food raw materials. In exchange for these relatively underpriced items, the USSR has imported from East Europe relatively overpriced machinery and industrial consumer goods, more often than not of poor quality and ill-suited to compete in international markets.[14]

Despite the relative decline in Soviet economic support, there still seems to be on the part of the USSR a willingness to forego economic benefits and bear the burden of subsidizing East European countries in return for "unconventional gains," i.e., continued political and military allegiance. Economic viability is, in fact, the foremost prerequisite for a politically stable East Europe; in this connection the state of the Polish economy will be a factor of outstanding importance for the rest of the region. Although the non-economic benefits appear to outweigh the economic costs of assistance to East Europe, at least for the time being, the Soviet leadership is facing some difficult choices among competing policy options. Such options include:

o   maintenance of the status quo, i.e., continuation of subsidies to East European economies (albeit on a generally smaller scale than in the 1970s);

o   cautious support of limited reform schemes in East Europe with a view to making the region's economies more efficient and ultimately less dependent on Soviet assistance; and

o   introduction of much-needed improvements in the CMEA mechanism so as to encourage truly multilateral cooperation and integration and to strengthen centripetal tendencies within the organization.

The choice of a path will eventually depend on several factors and circumstances, some of which are largely beyond the Soviet leadership's control, such as specific domestic developments in various East European countries.

The Crucial Economic Importance of West Europe to the USSR

The Kremlin leadership has long seen West Europe as the area par excellence in which Soviet influence and leverage can grow.[15]

To this end, the West European economic strategy of the USSR is conducted through a variety of channels ranging from international relations at the governmental level, to links between the CPSU and the West European communist parties, to business contacts with Western firms, bankers, and traders. In particular, the improvement in economic relations has been consistently pursued as a highly visible means of easing tensions and fostering regional detente.

The concept of the "divisibility of detente" and its more or less successful application to Soviet-West European relations have been playing a key role in shaping the Kremlin's course of action since the late 1970s. Selective detente has brought significant benefits to the USSR and has shown that, at least to a certain extent, relations between the USSR and the West European countries cannot be dealt with in isolation from the global Soviet-American confrontation.

In addition to focusing on increased West European dependence on Soviet raw materials deliveries, the Kremlin's approach is meant to loosen U.S.-West European ties and gradually to exclude the United States from Europe by taking advantage, inter alia, of growing U.S. interest toward the Pacific basin countries. It should be emphasized, however, that Soviet strategy is the outcome of the interaction of priorities, predicaments, and dilemmas rather than the expression of rigidly set and immutable aims and principles.

It seems to be beyond doubt that West Europe is a privileged partner that Moscow badly needs from both an economic and a technological viewpoint. Obviously, this is not to ignore that the Soviet-West European relationship is also beneficial to West European countries that, beyond any political and ideological considerations, have developed trade links with and extended credit lines to the USSR as well as East Europe for such prosaic motives as profits, markets, contracts, and job security.[16] On the whole, the basic systemic constraints involved in dealings between countries with different economic systems have played a far greater role than the changing prospects for detente.

Foreign trade traditionally makes a highly significant contribution to West Europe's gross national product and has been a factor of paramount importance in the economic growth of member countries of the EEC. The U.S. concerns about the security and strategic implications of East-West economic links are not fully and automatically shared by West European countries, which oftentimes view such links as a psychological reassurance against the risks of war that would be fought on European soil. This is especially true as regards the degree of West European dependence on the USSR for energy supplies. Oil and gas exports have helped the USSR to keep a major presence in West Europe and obtain substantial hard-currency earnings. Oil, in particular, has accounted for a very large percentage of the USSR's hard-currency receipts in recent years.

Soviet oil production has been growing at about 1 percent a year since the late 1970s and will probably meet the plan target of 630 million tons in 1985. Although significant differences still exist between Western analysts as regards the estimates of Soviet oil reserves as well as the assessments of the USSR's willingness and ability to boost output from the Siberian fields, in all likelihood Soviet oil production will continue to grow for several more years, probably through the end of this decade.

Western help to substantially enhance oil recovery techniques has been recently sought by the USSR. Through better performance and more adequate organization, the increase in West Siberian oil production could more than offset the decline in output in other regions. However, the inevitable rise in domestic demand for oil and energy in the USSR may well be a major constraining factor on Soviet ability to increase exports to pay for more imports, thereby making the question of substitution of gas for oil absolutely crucial.

West Europe, for her part, has been making remarkable progress toward the goal of reducing dependence upon imported oil and replacing oil as a fuel for generating electricity. Soviet natural gas production -- one of the brightest spots in the economy -- grows at a rate of 7 to 8 percent annually and should reach the planned goal for 1985 of 620-640 billion cubic meters. The USSR has adopted a policy which encourages West European countries to consider gas as a major alternative to oil. As a matter of fact, the development of the West European gas market has been supply-driven since the region is surrounded by large reserves in Algeria, Norway, and the USSR.

The Soviet share of natural gas in the West European energy market is gradually on the rise and the question of the USSR's growing role has become a highly controversial issue. The steady development of Soviet gas provides West European firms with opportunities to conclude contracts for more steel pipes, compressors, and gas purification plants, while serving the long-term interest of the USSR.

Despite the fact that Soviet gas is apparently more competitive against coal or nuclear power than Algerian and Norwegian gas, widespread concerns in West Europe for gas supply diversification will probably lead to keeping the USSR's share of the region's gas market relatively small. Altogether, some degree of dependence on Soviet oil and gas deliveries does not seem to be considered in West Europe a factor that substantially enhances the Kremlin's possibilities of putting pressure on West European policymakers.

The acquisition of advanced technology from West Europe is another facet of the East-West relationship that is of crucial importance to the USSR.[17] It may be interesting to recall that "substantial Western technological aid preceded the Bolshevik

Revolution by more than half a century."[18] During the Stalin era, the USSR embarked upon economic autarky, and inputs of Western know-how were drastically reduced.

In the post-Stalin years through the end of the 1960s and to a much greater extent in the 1970s, the USSR has gradually concentrated on imports of Western equipment embodying a high level of technology. Although it is almost impossible to establish to what extent foreign technology inputs have been effectively assimilated and diffused throughout the Soviet economy, it may safely be assumed that the infusion of Western technology has had a substantial impact on a number of Soviet industries, thereby contributing to the country's industrial growth.[19]

Despite some notable technological accomplishments on the part of the USSR, it is widely believed that very little progress in catching up with the West has been made by Soviet technology over the past three decades. There seems, in fact, to be no evidence of a significant diminution of the technological gap between the USSR and the West.

Since the West is likely to maintain for the foreseeable future its strong position with regard to both civil and military technologies, the improvement of the innovational system of socialism remains an urgent priority. Soviet policymakers face a difficult choice between improving economic performance by expanding technological imports -- mostly from West Europe because of U.S. sanctions and embargoes -- or turning inward by stressing the importance of indigenous solutions. As a matter of fact, there is a growing tendency in the USSR toward reducing dependence on foreign technology. It should also be borne in mind, that the influx of Western technology in this era of information revolution presents, in Soviet eyes, a danger of "ideological contamination" which should not be underestimated.

The West European Responses to Soviet Strategy

Any effective response to Soviet actions necessarily results from a combination of several factors involving peculiar and occasionally conflicting interests and goals on both sides of the Atlantic and within West Europe itself. Whatever the real chances of achieving a genuine all-European detente, the guidelines of the West European approach to the East-West relationship rest less on a basis of ideological priorities and national security implications than on economic and financial motives.

In other words, hard-currency liquidity and commercial considerations are likely to shape West European economic behavior vis-a-vis the USSR to a much greater extent than political commitments. The long-term stability of the East-West relationship in Europe is, in fact, closely tied to the fundamental willingness -- on the Soviet as well as on the West European side -- to stay on good enough terms to retain the advantages of mutual trade and industrial cooperation.

It remains an open question whether the benefits gained by West European public and private entities from economic and financial dealings with the USSR (and its East European allies) can always be balanced against the longer-term consideration of Western political and security objectives. The Soviet ability to use international economic links -- notably energy supplies to West Europe -- as an instrument for furthering the political goals of "Finlandization," should not be overrated, nor should any Western setback or hesitation be automatically considered to work to the USSR's advantage. Naturally this should not lead us to underestimate the urgent need for the Western allies to articulate a clear and consistent approach to East-West economic relations.

Despite recurring disagreements and clashes on specific issues between the United States and West Europe, opportunities do exist to reach reasonable compromises that take into account the different perspectives toward trade, cooperation, and detente with the USSR. Within this context, the central issue is whether economic warfare should be regarded by Western countries as an essential policy tool in international, or at least East-West, economic relations, or whether it should be rejected as the negation of the very principles according to which market economies are supposed to behave.[20] Of course, economic warfare is no novelty on the world scene and has been applied, more or less successfully, in the past to put pressure on governments in order to induce them to act or decide in a certain way.

A fresh and realistic approach to East-West relations ought to be based on a broad consensus between Western allies with regard to, inter alia, the qualitative aspects of trade policy, credit terms, and debt obligations, high-technology transfers and related sales, as well as sanctions and boycott measures. Throughout the 1970s and the early 1980s, permissive trade and credit policies have alternated with recurring threats and restrictions, which have ultimately hurt West European manufacturers and exporters with hardly any crippling effect on the Soviet economy.

A more significant role in bridging gaps between Western allies should be played by the intergovernmental institutions whose activities have a direct or indirect impact on the East-West economic relationship. Western countries should avail themselves to a greater degree of the multilateral framework provided by such institutions for the definition of concerted policies. The North Atlantic Treaty Organization (NATO) is concerned with the aspects of economic relations between East and West from the standpoint of security implications.

The issue of West European dependence on Soviet raw materials supplies inevitably assumes special relevance. In the Organization for Economic Cooperation and Development (OECD), the member countries' trade and financing policies toward the USSR and East Europe are investigated and discussed with a view to strengthening Western solidarity on critical issues. A significant step in this direction has been made, in the early 1980s, with respect to interest rates on long-term loans granted mainly to Third World importers but also to the USSR. In the 1970s, the USSR had access to credit from several West European countries on exceptionally favorable terms; according to the gentlemen's agreement recently reached within the OECD framework, "consensus rates" must reflect the evolution of market interest rates, without any undue preferential treatment of the USSR.

Measures for surveillance and control over Western exports to the USSR and its Warsaw Pact allies of equipment and technology with military and strategic relevance have been reviewed, over the past 35 years, within the framework of an informal organization, the Paris-based Coordinating Committee for Multilateral Exports Controls, usually known as COCOM. Among COCOM's main tasks there is, at present, the control of technology transfers, with special regard to the industrial techniques for the production of advanced weapons and strategic equipment.

Conflicts have periodically arisen, mostly between the United States and West European countries, over the inclusion of specific items in the lists administered by COCOM, and over the enforcement of the restrictive measures. In this connection, it is important to agree on a new list of high-technology exports and to adopt a more adequate system for the resolution of disputes. In the early 1980s, steps were taken to strengthen the COCOM mechanism in order to improve its activities and increase its efficiency.

The problems arising from the dependence of Western countries on non-OECD energy supplies and the necessity of relying on secure and diversified sources are also debated by the International Energy Agency (IEA), a body set up a decade ago within the OECD framework. Stability in world energy markets and security of energy supplies for member countries are among IEA's basic objectives.

A significant step toward establishing a more stable and predictable pattern for economic relations between the two halves of Europe, without damaging the West's security interests, would doubtless be taken with the conclusion of a framework agreement between the European Economic Community and the Council for Mutual Economic Assistance. Such an overall agreement should be followed by more detailed agreements between the community as such and each member country of the CMEA. In all likelihood, when the winds of global politics will eventually shift back toward a less strained relationship between East and West, the community's weight on the world scene will become greater.

Finally, West European as well as U.S. policymakers should keep in mind that the economy is but one of several components of the highly politicized Soviet society and that the ultimate question regards the future not only of the eastern half of Europe but of communist regimes and societies throughout the world. If the West as a whole still believes in its fundamental values, the intellectual and moral responses to the Soviet challenge could, in the end, prove to be of much greater consequence than outstanding economic performance or overwhelming force of arms.[21]

NOTES

1.   Zbigniew Brzezinski: "The Soviet Union: Her Aims, Problems and Challenges to the West," in The Conduct of East-West Relations in the 1980s, Part I, Adelphi Paper No. 189 (London: International Institute for Strategic Studies, 1984), p. 9. Recalling Khrushchev's challenge "We will bury you," Brzezinski emphasized it was not "a physical threat but a historic gauntlet, derived from misplaced confidence that American economic stagnation and Soviet economic dynamism would result in the emergence by the 1970s of the Soviet Union as the world's pre-eminent economic power."

2.   Pravda, April 27, 1984.

3.   Brezhnev's death marked the conclusion of an era in Soviet history. For a Marxist perspective, see Silviu Brucan: The Post-Brezhnev Era: An Insider's View (New York: Praeger, 1983).

4.   Thomas N. Bjorkman and Thomas J. Zamostny, "Soviet Politics and Strategy Toward the West: Three Cases," World Politics, Vol. XXXVI, no. 2 (January 1984), pp. 192-5.

5.   Guiseppe Schiavone, The Institutions of Comecon (London: MacMillan, 1981), p. 36.

6.   Statement by A.N. Manzhulo, Deputy Foreign Trade Minister, May 1983 in Moscow. See: "Mutually Advantageous Trade and Economic Cooperation Between the USSR and Other Countries: Results and Prospects," Foreign Trade, (July 1983), p. 37.

7.   Marshall I. Goldman, "Economic Problems in the Soviet Union," Current History, Vol. 82, no. 486 (October 1983), p. 339.

8.   For example, Academician Vadim Tragezvnikov - in an important article in Pravda (May 7, 1982) - pointed out that the poor performance of the Soviet economy over the past two and a half decades was largely due to "the complete absence of any competition and the virtual monopoly of producers in all fields."

9.   See the "Novosibirsk Paper," a supposedly confidential document, containing criticisms of the Soviet economic system, which was presented by Academician Tatiana Zaslavskaia at a seminar held in the USSR in April 1983. A few months later the text became known to the Western press and was first reported in The Washington Post, August 3, 1983. For details see Philip Hanson, "Discussion of Economic Reform in the USSR: the 'Novosibirsk Paper,' " Radio Liberty Research RL 356/83 (September 23, 1983).

10.   A slowdown in the growth rate of Soviet defense costs since the mid-1970s was reported by CIA analysts in early 1983. See Richard F. Kaufman, "Soviet Defense Trends," a staff study prepared for the use of the Subcommittee on International Trade, Finance, and Security Economics of the U.S. Congress Joint Economic Committee, September 1983, mimeo. Kaufman rightly criticizes (on p. 23 of his paper) the "tendency of equating the cost estimates with capabilities, misreading Soviet size for strength" and

68

thereby confusing "resource allocations with military power."

11. See Karen Dawisha and Philip Hanson, eds., <u>Soviet-East European Dilemmas</u> (London: Heinemann, 1981); and, Michael J. Sodaro and Sharon L. Wolchik, eds., <u>Foreign and Domestic Policy in Eastern Europe in the 1980s</u> (London: Macmillan, 1983).

12. U.N. Department of International Economic and Social Affairs, <u>World Economic Survey 1984: Current Trends and Policies in the World Economy</u> (New York: United Nations, 1984), p. 59.

13. Roger E. Kanet, "Modernizing Interaction within Eastern Europe," Charles Gati, ed., <u>The Politics of Modernization in Eastern Europe: Testing the Soviet Model</u> (Praeger: London, 1974) p. 295.

14. Jan Vanous, "East European Economic Slowdown," <u>Problems of Communism</u> (July-August 1982), pp. 1-19; Michael Marrese and Jan Vanous, <u>Implicit Subsidies and Non-Market Benefits in Soviet Trade with Eastern Europe</u> (Berkeley: University of California Institute of International Studies, 1983).

15. An in-depth analysis, mainly from a European perspective, of Soviet aims and policies with regard to Western Europe is to be found in Edwina Moreton and Gerald Segal, eds., <u>Soviet Strategy Toward Western Europe</u> (Winchester, Mass.: Allen & Unwin, 1984).

16. Paul Lendvai, "Relations Between Eastern and Western Europe: Prospects for Change: II," in <u>The Conduct of East-West Relations in the 1980s</u>, Part II, Adelphi Paper no. 190 (London: International Institute for Strategic Studies, 1984), p. 17.

17. Advanced technology may be acquired -- not by the USSR alone -- through a variety of methods ranging from fully licensed sales to illegal diversions and industrial espionage.

18. Richard N. Perle, "The Strategic Implications of West-East Technology Transfer," <u>Conduct of East-West Relations in the 1980s</u>, Part II, p. 20.

19. See Carl Gershman, "Selling Them the Rope: Business and the Soviets," <u>Commentary</u> (April 1979), pp. 35-45; Eugene Zaleski and Helgard Weinert, <u>Technology Transfer Between East and West</u> (Paris: OECD, 1980); Philip Hanson, <u>Trade and Technology in Soviet-Western Relations</u> (London: Macmillan, 1981).

20. For an updated analysis, see Reinhard Rode and Hanns-D. Jacobsen, eds., <u>Wirtschaftskrieg oder Entspannung? Eine politische Bilanz der Ost-West-Wirtschaftsbeziehungen</u> (Bonn: Verlag Neue Gesellschaft, 1984).

21. Giuseppe Schiavone, "Prospects for an EEC Policy Toward Eastern Europe," paper presented at a Seminar on "Common Trade Policy: the Comecon/CMEA," held in Maastricht, The Netherlands, 3-5 October 1984 (unpublished).

Chapter 6

PROPAGANDA AND PUBLIC OPINION IN SOVIET STRATEGY

Jonathan V. Luxmoore

"Decoupling" West Europe

The Renaissance exponent of Realpolitik, Machiavelli, wrote:

So these princes of ours whose power had been established many years, may not blame fortune for their losses. Their own indolence was to blame, because, having never imagined when times were quiet that they could change, when adversity came their first thoughts were of flight and not of resistance.[1]

Preparedness and the prompt identification of threats have always been the principal obligations of societies intending to remain free. There is ample evidence that for much of the twentieth century, the Soviet Union has been working to bring within its power the free democratic states of West Europe. If this evidence is accepted, the attractiveness of the democratic West European states would easily be explained.

West Europe remains the hub of a successful world economic order. It is the site of an opposing military alliance, the heartland of an antipathetic liberal capitalist ideology and the magnetic center of attraction for the fissiparous and centrifugal forces at work within the Soviet Union's immediate sphere of influence.

To secure eventual control, however, the leaders of the Soviet Union must first succeed in "decoupling" West Europe from its American protector, and to do so it must destroy the relationships, values, beliefs, and priorities which provide the principal pillars of the trans-Atlantic link.

If the long-term global strategy of Moscow has not changed, the methods and tactics used in its pursuit have been subject to constant review, in accordance with changing circumstances and the availability of exploitable opportunities.

In the pursuit of its strategy, the Soviet Union has encountered in West Europe democratic political systems vulnerable to every conceivable form of pressure and manipulation. Forms of pressure and manipulation which might involve the USSR in direct conflict with its superpower rival have been avoided.

But even within this limitation, the open nature of West European society has provided Moscow with a wide range of opportunities for furthering its aims. The free press, the considerable freedom of peace movements to demonstrate and otherwise express their views, the left-wing orientation of many politicians and labor leaders -- these are all manifestations of West Europe's vulnerability to Moscow's efforts to gain influence and promote its policies.

Given its implacable hostility to any manifestations of democracy at home, the skill and alacrity with which Moscow has sought to influence West Europe's decision-makers and to control the consciousness of European populations, by means of the democratic process, have been all the more remarkable.[2] Moscow has correctly identified the prevailing trends which have helped to shape the course of events; it has understood and exploited the hopes and aspirations, the fears and neuroses, of West European citizens.

Moscow knows that in an ideal world West Europe would be free to enjoy the fruits of its prosperity and freedom, unhampered by the responsibilities of defense preparedness and secure within an international community composed of like-minded leaders obedient to the same system of rights and obligations.

So too, Moscow has identified the powerful tendency in West Europe to evade reality, to seek appeasement, and to imagine a world governed by reason and fair play, in which real conflicts of interest, real threats and real dangers do not exist, and all bilateral and multilateral disputes are attributable to no more than a lack of knowledge and understanding, or to the antics of irresponsible and pugnacious politicians.

Soviet strategy has never existed in a vacuum. It has attempted instead to anticipate and exploit movements in public opinion and the changing perceptions of decision-makers. The harnessing of such trends to produce political results has played a central part in the Soviet Union's political campaigns.

In this way, the basic components of Moscow's political strategy against West Europe reveal as much about the disposition of the USSR's intended victims as they do about the cynicism and artfulness of their designers.

The strategy of "peaceful coexistence" which was enunciated by Khrushchev in the 1950s -- dynamic strategy, which enabled the Soviet Union to preserve the outward forms of cooperation whilst pursuing its ideological struggle by all available means -- could not have proved credible had its principal assumptions not already enjoyed a substantial constituency in West Europe.

East-West Relations: Detente

The same was true with the later theories of East-West detente. Disillusioned and alarmed by the years of Cold War, the West Europeans knew that lasting peace and security would only be secured if rational, peace-loving, and honest qualities could be discerned in the Soviet leadership. They presupposed a receptiveness on the USSR's part to liberalizing influences, of the kind which would be generated by peaceful economic, cultural, scientific, and educational contacts with the West. They required the kind of pluralism which would be based upon the existence of rival ideas about internal reform and foreign policy, and an element of accountability to "public opinion," of which the Soviet Communist Party was somehow deemed to be representative.

To encourage the belief that these factors existed, the Soviet Union had merely to create evidence which would satisfy the wishful thinking of West European appeasers. How, indeed, could the Soviet Union fail to be seen in such a positive light? If the Soviet Union were genuinely deceitful and untrustworthy -- an "evil empire," whose pledges and undertakings were worthless -- what possible value could there be in reaching agreements with it? If the Soviet Union truly symbolized the abuse of human freedoms and the repression of national rights, how could the West withstand the grave moral debilitation incurred by trading and cooperating with it? If the Soviet Union were really an aggressive and expansionist power, could the West ever be satisfied with anything less than the most exorbitant expenditure for defense?

Because the credibility of long-established policies, a wealth of personal and departmental reputations, and all hopes for a peaceful, indolent future have come to rest upon such thinking, it is hardly surprising that detente remains a concept cherished by all shades of political opinion in West Europe. This thinking reflects the premises and postulates upon which the West's methodology of East-West relations has been constructed. The possibility of detente and peaceful cooperation between ideologically antagonistic power blocs is one such premise; another is that current procedures for arms control will produce security and confidence. Another premise is that trade will have a liberalizing effect upon the entrenched power of the Soviet Communist Party; still another is that there can be faith in signed agreements and statements of intent.

Whilst the attendant problems and difficulties are openly acknowledged, these premises and postulates are rarely submitted to re-examination and reappraisal. Should they be discredited in the cold light of past experience, the consequences would be too alarming to contemplate.

This bureaucraticization of Western statecraft gives preference to long-established practices and renders the task of reexamining and re-appraising existing policies an onerous one. It becomes increasingly difficult to reconcile the present conduct of East-West relations with what is known, on the basis of firm evidence, of the motives and promptings of the East European and Soviet governments -- certainly in a manner likely to convince a sceptical Western public. This, in turn, creates pressure for public opinion to be excluded from the policymaking process and denied access to information which would enable it to support or oppose policies and decisions in a constructive and beneficial way. The Western media are barred from the review sessions of the Conference on Security and Co-operation in Europe (CSCE). The U.S. government withholds evidence of the Soviet Union's violation of past arms control agreements from its own population, in order not to jeopardize the pursuit of new agreements.[3] Public opinion is left confused and suspicious, and ever more vulnerable to the illusions and uncertainties which can be encouraged and exploited by Soviet propaganda.

As it has sought to weaken the West's powers of perception and response, the Soviet Union has continued to promote the notion of a status quo in East-West relations. It is a notion eagerly espoused by Western policymakers, for whom it justifies, among other things, the withholding of support from the proponents of political change, from dispossessed minority groups, from innovators in the field of strategy, and from those seeking to link the conduct of East-West trade and other forms of cooperation with an improvement in the Soviet Union's human rights record.

In reality, the status quo of detente remains for Moscow as it has always been: a dynamic process which provides the Soviet Union with an ideal framework in which to pursue its political strategy against West Europe. Moscow makes no secret of its distinction between its official relations with Western governments on the one hand, which are subject to customary diplomatic constraints, and its relations with communist parties, indigenous liberation movements, and progressive groups on the other, in its dealings with which it continues to claim a free hand. This distinction lies at the heart of its interpretation of detente.

Soviet Propaganda: Advantages of the Helsinki Final Act

How, then, has Moscow succeeded in encouraging and exploiting such developments? One of the principal factors in its success has been a vast imbalance in the channels of information and influence available to the governments of East and West, and it is in this area that many of the key illusions and uncertainties of the West Europeans have been most apparent. For the West European governments, provisions for East-West cooperation in the fields of information, culture, and education -- such as those which were agreed under the Helsinki Final Act of 1975 -- have always had a high priority. It was in these fields that the best prospects for peaceful change and beneficial cooperation were believed to lie.

The Final Act itself is an important case in point, since the specific provisions agreed upon appeared to offer the means of bypassing official state mechanisms and providing Western ideas and values with direct access to the peoples of the Soviet Union and East Europe. Did they not, after all, include an acknowledgement of "the essential and influential role of the press, radio, television, cinema, and news agencies, and of journalists working in these fields?" Did they not embody an undertaking to "facilitate the improvement" necessary in the circulation of newspapers and other printed matter?

These provisions would enhance the normative status of the Universal Declaration of Human Rights, which guarantees to all citizens the right "to seek, receive, or impart information and ideas through any media and regardless of frontiers."[4] The logic of the situation demanded that short-term sticking points -- in the practical exercise of human rights, for example -- be avoided, so as not to jeopardize the more important long-term advantages likely to be achieved by the infusion of liberalizing Western influences.

In the political climate of the late 1970s, it seemed a sensible bargain. To be able to propagate the values of freedom and human dignity unhindered, and in so doing to be able to present accurate images of both Western and Communist societies, was clearly a central prerequisite for real and lasting progress.

Could any program of beneficial change in the societies of the Soviet Union and East Europe prove effective unless an objective knowledge of the facts were available to its proponents? Could a reasoned assessment of the practical possibilities be made whilst information remained the preserve of the state authorities, who could withhold and manipulate the facts at will, obscure the extent of the Soviet Union's international undertakings and constitutional provisions, conceal their discrepancy with the actual conduct of the state, deny their citizens knowledge of national cultures and traditions predating the Communist era, and deprive their audience of the means of distinguishing truth from falsehood in the information continuously being fed to it by state propagandists?

To be able to offer evidence of the West's pacific intentions and to refute Soviet allegations regarding Western society's "crisis of confidence," "loss of unity," and "collective inertia" would similarly help to deprive the Soviet Union of justification for its increased arms expenditure, its campaigns of intimidation, its ideological struggles, and its political repressions at home.

In any case, the Helsinki bargain was never kept. Since 1975, the Soviet Union has taken full advantage of the freedom of communication practiced in the West to disseminate its propaganda and disinformation -- without any gesture of genuine reciprocation. It has exploited the Final Act's emphasis upon "normal channels," which enables its propagandists to use the multifarious, uncontrolled media outlets in West Europe, whilst demanding that all Western information remain subject to their own "normal" monopoly at home. Moscow has exploited the familiar West European tendency to self-effacement and self-censorship in the field of information exchanges, together with a distaste for the competitive business of propaganda and the poor public relations existing between the governments and electorates with regard to foreign affairs.

Moscow has benefited in a host of other ways from the Helsinki process, over 60 percent of the costs of which are met by the Western nations. It has contrived to have the CSCE's security aspects removed from the mainstream of the process, and it has exploited the unwillingness of West European delegates, preoccupied with their desire to avoid confrontation, to press it appropriately on the question of implementation.

The Kremlin has also helped to create confusion in West European minds over the question of recognition of the postwar division of Europe, which the CSCE is wrongly held to have brought about. In reality, such an interpretation is expressly rejected in the Final Act; the very raison d' etre of such a process depends upon a willingness to seek the gradual elimination of such divisions. Yet the strident criticism levelled against recent attempts to clarify the issue testifies to the extent to which the expansionist power of the Soviet Union has come to be regarded as an inevitable and irreversible force in the contemporary world.

When the British Prime Minister, Margaret Thatcher, expressed her belief to the House of Commons, several months before the opening of the CSCE's Madrid meeting, that the West should be doing much more, by means of constructive propaganda, to promote liberal change in the societies of the Soviet Union and East Europe, she was widely criticized for an approach which, in the words of the managing director of the BBC's External Services, "appeared counter-productive and dishonest."[5]

Power of the Soviet Disinformation Apparatus

Aided by the West's reticence, the Soviet Union continues to profit from a propaganda apparatus of vast proportions. It has over 500 journalists working abroad, with open access to West European politicians and people. The Novosti press agency alone remains in regular contact with West European publishers and editors, and supplies a large range of syndicated press articles. Soviet publications are distributed openly and cheaply to schools and colleges in the relevant languages. These conditions are not reciprocated by the Soviet bloc. Although the late 1970s saw some tentative improvements in the working conditions of Western journalists in certain countries, these have been offset by subsequent restraints -- for example, on contacts with dissident groups like the 1982 Moscow hunger-strikers and the independent peace group -- and by recent visa restrictions and expulsions.

Currently, the only officially approved Western equivalent to the Soviet newspapers and journals permitted to circulate in the West are the principal Communist Party organs, such as the French l' Humanite, the German Unsere Zeit, and the British Morning Star, and a few government-sponsored publications, such as the German Guten Tag and the British Anglia. The contents of the latter, parts of which are sent to the Soviet Union for translation into Russian, are highly selective and do not include political or other controversial issues.

In the field of radio broadcasting, generally regarded as the most important single medium of communication, the Soviet Union maintains the most extensive network in the world. Its output includes 2,180 hours of original external broadcasts in 83 languages every week. The annual operating cost of Radio Moscow alone was estimated in 1982 to be $700 million. Its English-language "World Service," which was launched in 1978, claims to attract up to 1,000 letters each day in response to its round-the-clock broadcasts. As in the field of printed information, these efforts are not reciprocated. Moscow currently operates a massive network of some 3,000 jamming transmitters throughout the Soviet Union, the operating costs of which were estimated as long ago as 1971 to be already far in excess of that of the Soviet Union's own international broadcasts. Such a state of affairs renders nonsensical the Soviet Union's approval, under the terms of the Helsinki Final Act, of "the expansion in the dissemination of information broadcast by radio," and its expression of "hope for the continuation of this process, so as to meet the interests of mutual understanding among peoples."[6]

This propaganda imbalance has greatly helped the Soviet Union in its efforts to influence West European public opinion over such issues as nuclear deterrence, membership in the North Atlantic Treaty Organization (NATO), East-West negotiations, and the protection of Europe's vital interests in the Third World. It has also enabled Moscow to have some impact on the course of national elections, in which the loss of consensus in West Germany and Britain over the fundamental issues of defense and foreign policy, and the latent anti-American sentiments of Left and Right alike, arising in some cases from fears of American unreliability and a pool of petty resentments, have been similarly exploited.

In recent years, Moscow has devoted increasing attention to the new manifestations of disaffection and alienation within the

West European community. In several cases, groups who have used the European peace movement as a platform for their causes, such as anti-nuclear activists, ecologists, feminists, radical educationists, ethnic minority militants, and church members, have provided a receptive audience for Soviet propaganda. Moscow's ability to harness and exploit the empathy of such groups was underlined by the unexpected strength of the campaign against NATO's nuclear modernization program in the early 1980s. Its influence almost certainly played a part in the successful campaign against the deployment of enhanced radiation weapons (the so-called "neutron bomb") in the late 1970s, and it may well prove instrumental in the withholding of European support from the U.S. President's Strategic Defense Initiative.

Moscow has not, however, neglected what it still professes to regard as the industrial vanguard of the revolutionary process. In this respect, the role of the Soviet Union during the strike by the British National Union of Mineworkers (NUM) is instructive. In addition to Moscow's pledges of "moral and material support," official sources also hinted during October 1984 that the Soviet Union would consider suspending the delivery of contracted fuel supplies to Britain, as a gesture of political solidarity.[7] Moscow's intention to do so was later denied. But the NUM had already been the beneficiary of Soviet funds, ostensibly collected on the initiative of Ukranian trade unions, and of highly publicized holidays in the Soviet Union for British workers and their families in sympathy for the striking NUM miners. Moscow continues to provide a platform for other British trade union activists, thereby ensuring that its appeal amongst embittered and disaffected industrial workers remains strong.

However varied their principal targets may be, Soviet propaganda and disinformation yield continual dividends. Moscow's success in exploiting the gullibility and credulity of the West European media to obscure its alleged role in the attempted assassinaton of Pope John Paul II in May 1981, and in sowing doubts about its culpability for destroying the South Korean civilian airliner on September 1, 1983, are classic examples of the Soviet Union's disinformation apparatus at work.[8] A further example concerns its successful depiction of General Jaruzelski's imposition of martial law in Poland as the act of a Polish patriot anxious to preserve his country from a worse fate. Moscow has also sought to depict NATO's Intermediate-Range Nuclear Forces (INF) modernization program, in the face of plain evidence to the contrary, as an American decision, imposed on reluctant Europeans.

It continues to leak "evidence" of political developments within the Kremlin which appear favorable to West Europe. In the months following Brezhnev's death, it successfully created an image of his successor, Andropov, as a progressive reformer and devotee of contemporary Western culture, an image which confirmed the Western media's conviction that a struggle was taking place, between the younger, "liberal" elements within the Soviet leadership and a more rigid old guard, which was certain to lead in the direction of liberalization and stability if its dimensions were adequately understood and its protagonists accorded suitable recognition in the West.

Wishful Thinking in the West

The Soviet Union's depiction of events admirably suits the longing of West Europeans for signs of a relaxation in East-West tensions which will confirm the practicability of a genuine detente. These Europeans argue that if detente is to retain its status as a fundamental premise for Western policies, we must imagine a Soviet Union (if one does not already exist) which will respond in an appropriate manner. If there is no substantive evidence that detente has already achieved beneficial results, we must create new evidence capable of absolving us of past errors of judgment. If the interests of West Europe seem irreconcilable with the stated objectives of the Soviet Union, we must change our perception of those interests and objectives so that they become reconcilable. If certain of our allies are less inclined to ad hoc concessions and compromises, we must ensure that our relationship with those allies does not impede our continuing pursuit of detente. If responsive and receptive Soviet leaders do not come forward of their own accord, we must summon them into existence.

The visit to Britain of Mikhail Gorbachev, then a senior member of the Soviet Politburo, at the head of a 30-strong delegation in December 1984, provided a classic example of Moscow's ability to exploit the wishful thinking of West Europeans in such directions, implicitly casting doubt upon the pledge of the British Prime Minister after her re-election in 1983 that her government would deal with the Soviet Union "not as one would like it, but as it is."[9] Gorbachev's visit, as a guest of the British branch of the Inter-Parliamentary Union, was regarded as a valuable opportunity for the Kremlin's "heir-apparent" to gain experience and knowledge of the West.

If the visit of a senior Politburo member could enable Britain to play a leading role in reducing international tensions and promoting understanding, Gorbachev seemed the perfect man for the part. Was he not the principal representative of a rising liberal, progressive, reformist generation of Soviet leaders, noted for their pragmatism, and for their opposition to the dogmatism of the Kremlin's old guard? Had he not been heard to advocate a "return to detente," "constructive dialogue," "change for the better," "goodwill and determination" in East-West relations? The Moscow correspondent of The Times wrote:

> Mr. Gorbachev is the child of the apparatus he hopes to reform. . . . He and his generation are feeling their way forward. Whether the conservative or the reformer in Gorbachev comes to the fore, suspicion or trust, hostility or dialogue, could very largely depend on how he reacts to the West, and how the West reacts to him.[10]

In the event, Gorbachev did not disappoint his British audience. His message was one of "goodwill and good intentions." He promised that an increase in Anglo-Soviet trade to the tune of 40-50 percent would be forthcoming, together with some improvement in the prospects for arms control, provided that West Europe remained steadfast in its opposition to the Strategic Defense Initiative endorsed by President Reagan, an issue over which Britain and the Soviet Union were said to share much common ground. These gestures found a ready response on the British side.

In broadcasts by the BBC, Gorbachev was described as a "fellow parliamentarian" and "presidential contender." Such words as "charismatic" and "impressive" were constantly in the air. Gorbachev dined at Hampton Court Palace, visited the British Parliament, and enjoyed a guided tour of memorials and sites associated with the life and work of Karl Marx in London. The visit received press attention throughout, of the kind similar to, and perhaps even greater than, that usually reserved for visiting heads of state. A daily account was given of Gorbachev's activities, and his photograph appeared on the front pages of British newspapers.

How, then, does the optimistic speculation which greeted the visit measure up about what is known about the life and work of Gorbachev himself? It is known, for example, that Gorbachev is young, that he has obtained two university degrees, that his personal background is that of the post-Stalin generation, and that he has maintained an interest in the areas of ideology and agriculture. Yet it is not known which precise offices and responsibilities he currently holds. Should some measure of speculation be justified, furthermore, in the absence of verifiable information, does not the remarkable speed of Gorbachev's rise in the Communist Party apparatus reveal, far from progressive or reformist views, an unusually rigid and reliable adherence to the Party's line? It is known that, with his wife, Raisa, at his side, Gorbachev is said to present the "human face" of the Soviet Politburo. Yet it is not even known whether the couple has children.

We clearly need to be alert to the difficulties and dangers which are certain to arise when optimistic speculation, the product of wishful thinking and a myopic vision of Europe's security interests, provide the basis for policy decisions and new political and diplomatic initiatives. The figure of Mikhail Gorbachev serves as a powerful focus for the hopes and aspirations of West Europeans, longing for signs of relaxation and a reaffirmation of detente. As a man, Gorbachev is plain to see: tall, robust, and endowed with sartorial elegance. As a liberal, progressive reformer and friend of the West, Gorbachev is, for all practical purposes, a figment of Western imagination. The confusion of many West Europeans about the nature and aims of Soviet leaders makes it virtually impossible to think rationally about the requirements of an adequate defense.

West Europe's overwhelming preoccupation with purely military considerations has led it to neglect the more insidious dangers arising from the Soviet Union's political strategy. Just as an equation based on erroneous data cannot work, so any political relationship based upon false premises or an artificial interpretation of the partner's motives must, sooner or later, lead to disaster. The creeping confusion and despondency which Machiavelli regarded half a millenium ago as the principal tool of cynical and artful rulers are increasingly evident in West Europe's political relationship with the Soviet Union. They represent, in short, the principal achievement of the Soviet Union's political strategy.

NOTES

1. Niccolo Machiavelli, Il Principe, XXIV; English edition, London, 1975.

2. For a recent assessment, see Richard Pipes, "How Vulnerable is the West?" in Survey, Vol. 28, no. 2.

3. See, for example, Newsweek, October 22, 1984, and The Times, October 1, 1984.

4. The Conference on Security and Co-operation in Europe, Final Act; Command 6198, HMSO., London, 1975. The International Bill of Rights; Office of Public Information, United Nations, New York, 1978.

5. See The Times, May 6, 1980. For the text of Mrs. Thatcher's subsequent reply, see Parliamentary Debates (Hansards), Fifth Series, Vol. 985, June 5, 1980.

6. See the BBC Annual Report and Handbook 1984, London, 1983; Christopher Perzanowski, "Russia's Radio Putsch," in The National Review, April 15, 1983; Paul Lendvai, The Bureaucracy of Truth: How Communist Governments Manage the News; Andre Deutsch, London, 1982; and Report of the Advisory Commission on Public Diplomacy; Washington, D.C., January 1984.

7. The Times, October 31, 1984.

8. The role of the Soviet disinformation in the first case is discussed in Paul Henze, "The Plot to Kill the Pope," in Survey, Vol. 27, no. 118-119, Autumn-Winter 1983. A detailed but anonymous article in the international bimonthly journal Defence Attache, published in mid-1984, purported to produce evidence that KAL 007 was on an espionage mission, coordinated by U.S. intelligence, at the time of its fateful flight over Sakhalin on August 31, 1983. Korean Air Lines was subsequently awarded substantial damages against the journal's publishers, according to International Herald Tribune, November 20, 1984.

9. Address at British Embassy in Washington, The Times, September 30, 1983.

10. The Times, December 13, 1984.

Chapter 7

TERRORISM IN SOVIET STRATEGY

Yonah Alexander

State Sponsored Terrorism as Defined and Employed

The Soviet Union is employing "state-sponsored terrorism" in Europe. Soviet propaganda citing "peace struggles" and "freedom fighters" obscures the role that Soviet training, weapons, money, and political encouragement provided to terrorists are playing in destabilizing societies in West Europe. Soviet assistance is usually covert or indirect, and usually officially denied.[1]

A working definition in the strategic context suggests that "state-sponsored terrorism" is:

> The deliberate employment of violence or the threat of use of violence by sovereign states or sub-national groups encouraged or assisted by sovereign states to attain strategic and political objectives by acts in violation of the law intended to create overwhelming fear in a target population larger than the civilian or military victims attacked or threatened.[2]

It is further suggested that recent history indicates:

> The main goal of "state-sponsored terrorism" now at the end of the twentieth century is to undermine the psycho-social stability and political governability of pluralist states with representative governments.[3]

The threatened and actual resort to ideological and political violence for the purpose of achieving limited or broad realistic or imaginary goals by both established regimes and opposition forces is not new in the history of Europe. Ancient civilizations such as Greece and Rome have, in the struggle for power with other nations, utilized extralegal, psychological, and physical force. For example, they, as well as other European maritime states between the sixteenth and late eighteenth centuries, found it expedient to employ pirates, or privateers, to terrorize the seas for the purpose of advancing some national policy objectives. Similarly, terrorism was practiced by the party in power in France during the Revolution of 1789-1794, including the government-established "reign of terror" in 1793-1794.

Moreover, terrorism from "below" utilized by sub-state groups against their own governments, as well as against other social organizations, became popular in the nineteenth and into the early years of the twentieth century. Cases in point are the activities of the Norodnaya Volya movement targeting Imperial Russia; the use of violence by nationalistic groups such as the Irish, Macedonians, Serbs, and Armenians, all struggling for sovereign existence; and the resort to "propaganda by the deed," as a strategy of political action by radicals and anarchists determined to overthrow the established order of states.

While these groups failed in achieving their strategic aims, nonetheless they attained some tactical success. Some of the victims of terrorist assassination are Tsar Alexander II in 1881, French President Carnot in 1894, Spain's Prime Minister in 1897, Austria's Empress Elizabeth (Zita) in 1898, and Italy's King Umberto in 1900. Regicide and other terrorist acts continued in several European countries, including Russia and Spain, until 1914, but abated in Central and West Europe.

Terrorists of Today and Their Targets

During World War II, ideological and political violence was undertaken by various European resistance movements and directed against the Nazi occupiers. But it was not until the late 1960s and the 1970s that Europe, particularly West Europe, led all other regions in the world in incidences of terrorist activities.

Unique political circumstances led to this development: the defeat of the Arab states in the June 1967 war and the subsequent rise in Palestinian terrorism abroad; the Vietnam War and the widespread demonstrations against it; and the Paris student revolt of 1968.

These circumstances, coupled with developments in modern technology, particularly inexpensive and convenient travel and communication facilities, have contributed to the rise of European imitators of ideologically motivated extremist movements in the Third World, and to the strengthening of indigenous European ethnic and separatist groups.[4]

Indeed, over 200 domestic and foreign terrorist groups have been active in Europe since the late 1960s. Among the most publicized European movements are the Irish Republican Army

(IRA), a militant Catholic movement which is struggling for the unification to the Irish Republic of the predominately Protestant, British-ruled province of Northern Ireland (Ulster); the Red Army Faction (RAF), an extremist urban group in West Germany aiming to overthrow capitalism and the present parliamentary system in the country; the Red Brigades (Brigate Rosse), a radical Marxist movement in Italy determined to create a communist state and destroy the "capitalistic domination" of the government; Basque Nation and Liberty (Euzkadi ta Azkatasuma or ETA), a clandestine militant movement seeking a separate Basque homeland in Spain; the Communist Combatant Cells of Belgium, which has declared "class war" against NATO and "international imperialism;" Direct Action of France, an extremist left-wing group formed to attack NATO interests; Portugal's Popular Forces of April 25 (FP-25), which advocates armed revolution against Western capitalism; and the People's Revolutionary Struggle, the largest terrorist organization in Greece.[5]

In addition to indigenous European groups, a great variety of foreign movements operate in the region unilaterally or in cooperation with other bodies. Typical are the activities of the Abu Nidal Faction (Fatah Revolutionary Council), the Popular Front for the Liberation of Palestine (PFLP), the United Red Army, and the Armenian Secret Army for the Liberation of Armenia (ASALA).[6]

American citizens have been a major target of international terrorist incidents in Europe. For example, in 1982, 45 percent of all attacks directed against Americans worldwide occurred in West Europe -- primarily in West Germany (77), Italy (37), and Greece (24). Moreover, international terrorist acts in Europe directed against U.S. diplomatic and military facilities and personnel between 1974 and the end of 1983 numbered 110. The majority of incidents occurred in Turkey (36), Greece (35), and West Germany (30). Other countries that experienced anti-American terrorism include Italy, France, and the Netherlands.[7]

For instance, in 1981 alone, there were a total of fifteen terrorist attacks against U.S. Army installations in West Germany. The Commander of U.S. Army Forces in Europe, General Frederick Kroesen, and three others, were injured in an anti-tank grenade attack against their armor-plated car near Heidelberg. The Red Army Faction, in cooperation with the Gudrez Enslin Commando group, claimed responsibility for the incident and called for attacks on "the centers, the bases and the strategists of the American military machine."[8]

During the same year, terrorists kidnapped U.S. Army Brig. Gen. James Dozier, attached to NATO's Southern Headquarters Command, from his home in Verona, Italy. The Red Brigades, identifying themselves as part of an "organization of Communist combat" engaged in a war against "NATO's heartland in Western

Europe," held General Dozier captive for 42 days. In a communique issued by the terrorists after his release by a special Italian police squad ("Leatherheads"), the Red Brigades vowed that "the liberation of Dozier will not succeed in stopping the current revolutionary progress."[9]

In 1984 and 1985, attacks directed against U.S. and NATO-related targets intensified. Some examples worthy of mention are the attack on a U.S. Army depot in Frankfurt, by the Red Army Faction; the bombing in Belgium of NATO's oil pipeline network for Central Europe, by the Communist Combatant Cells; the bombing of an army draft office in Holland, by the Northern Terror Front; the assassination of French defense official General Rene Augran, by members of Direct Action; the murder of prominent German arms businessman Ernst Zimmerman, by a squad of the Red Army Faction; the shelling of NATO warships in Lisbon harbor by FP-25; and the bombing perpetrated by the National Front of a bar frequented by U.S. servicemen in Greece.

Admittedly, the record of the incidence of ideological and political violence directed against U.S. military and NATO-related targets in Europe is relatively small in comparison to the total of terrorist attacks on other targets in the world. Yet, the impact of anti-military terrorism is more accurately measured in terms of the amount of attention received and the atmosphere of fear generated.

Moreover, although the tactical successes of terrorist activities have been limited to short-range goals, terrorism is likely to persist and grow as a form of political expression. Freelance terrorist groups for hire to governments may emerge, and terrorists may acquire an unprecedented capacity for violence and disruption.[10]

Moscow's Support for Terrorism

It is likely that changing European political, economic, and social patterns in domestic and international situations over the next two decades might give rise to pressure and tension that could motivate terrorists, with direct and indirect Soviet support, to engage in conventional and unconventional attacks directed both at civilian and military targets.

Moscow's justification of the use of terrorism as a legitimate political tool has its ideological roots in the works of the founders of orthodox Marxism-Leninism and other prominent communist authors. To a greater or lesser extent they all advocated the employment of confrontation tactics, including terrorism, for achieving communist aims.

In Das Kapital Marx asserted: "Force (Gewalt) is the midwife of an old society which is pregnant with a new one. Gewalt is an economic factor (Potenz)." This conviction persisted not only in Marx's later writings but also, with some modifications, in the works of Lenin. He, too, held that the revolutionary struggle might appropriately include terrorism. [11] Thus, the Soviet commitment to revolutionary violence is very deep and is enshrined in the doctrinal literature passed on systematically to successive generations of Communist Party leaders.

To be sure, as a superpower with political, diplomatic, economic, and military interests all over the world, the Soviet Union itself has become increasingly vulnerable to various forms of terrorism. One need only mention the hijacking of Soviet aircraft, the kidnapping and assassination of Soviet officials and diplomats, and the bombing of Soviet embassies and trade missions. Nonetheless, Moscow clearly uses terrorism as a major tool in its global strategy.

It was not until the 1960s that Moscow became intimately involved with the training of communist and non-communist terrorist and insurgent groups throughout the world. Two major factors contributed to the Kremlin's determination to play a more active role. First the Kremlin realized that nuclear war with the United States was virtually unthinkable. Second, many revolutionary movements adopted a certain comradeship with each other and with Moscow in their struggle against imperialism and capitalism and for the liberation of "dependent peoples."

By the 1970s, low-level conflict, whether backed directly or indirectly by the Soviet Union or independently initiated, appeared to have become an indispensable tactical and strategic tool in the Soviet struggle for power and influence within and among nations. Europe received major emphasis in the development of Soviet links with terrorist groups.

From the first Marxist-Leninist revolution against Czarism -- when more than a thousand terrorist acts were perpetrated in Trans-Caucasia alone -- to the present day, Moscow-oriented communism has encouraged and assisted terrorist groups in Europe that follow a strict party line and are highly centralized. Terrorist movements with less party discipline and control, including the New Left, and even Trotskyists (working to advance international communism while remaining hostile to the Soviet Union) have also, on occasion, received some support when their violence destabilized Soviet target societies. Moreover, from considerations of political expedience rather than ideological solidarity, a wide range of extremist groups -- sectarian, nationalist, separatist, and anarchist -- have frequently been supported by the Soviet Union. [12]

Notwithstanding such ideological differences, the Soviet Union does not hesitate to provide assistance to a multitude of groups. In relying upon terrorism as an instrument of foreign policy, Moscow seems to aim, in the 1980s, at achieving strategic ends in circumstances where the use of conventional armed forces is deemed either inappropriate, ineffective, too risky, or too difficult.

The broad goals the Soviet Union hopes to achieve from terrorism include: Regaining irredentist territories in the Soviet orbit (as in Turkey); weakening the political, economic, and military infrastructure of anti-Soviet alliances such as NATO; frustrating efforts of non-NATO countries (such as Spain) from joining the alliance; and, destabilizing relatively prosperous West Europe so that its stability and prosperity will be less of an attraction to East Europeans.

The Soviet Union also involves European terrorist groups in attacking persons considered by the Kremlin to be "mortal enemies" of communism and the USSR. The most significant example is the attempt by a Turkish terrorist to assassinate Pope John Paul II on May 13, 1981. As the trial of the assailant Ali Agca has shown, the connection between Agca and the KGB-dominated Bulgarian secret service is clear.[13]

Despite the often murky nature of the evidence, it is obvious that there exists a carefully developed infrastructure which serves Moscow's foreign policy objectives in Europe and elsewhere.[14] The International Department of the Central Committee of the Communist Party of the Soviet Union, the Soviet Security Agency (KGB), and Soviet Military Intelligence (GRU) have played the major roles in building and guiding this operational network. Of the three organs, the party's International Department, headed by Boris Ponomarev, is believed to be the most important Soviet agency for the support of terrorism. It has consistently promoted widespread revolutionary violence abroad even while taking care to project the illusory image that the USSR has been abiding by the spirit of "peaceful coexistence."

The KGB, headed by Yuri Andropov for 15 years before he became chief of the Soviet Communist Party and Soviet State, has established a special section at its Moscow headquarters for the recruiting and training of revolutionaries. The Third Department of the GRU, in close cooperation with the KGB, provides direct military instruction. It is estimated that the Soviet Union spends more than $20 million per year on such training within the country.

The Kremlin has set up an elaborate infrastructure of over forty training camps within the Soviet Union. The camps in Moscow, Tashkent, Batum on the Black Sea, Odessa, Baku, Simferopol (a major base known for housing the Soviet Academy for Military Training), and the Vistral Academy provide specialized training for terrorists and insurgents. At these locations the techniques of guerrilla warfare and other skills -- including the use of explosives, mining of transportation routes, commando field tactics, and combat capabilities of shoulder-fired rockets -- are being taught to many revolutionaries.

Of particular concern are reports that the USSR is stepping up the use and training of SPETSNAZ (Spetsnaznacheniya), the special commando units that are charged with missions too sensitive for regular Soviet military forces. This group stresses the use of behind-the-lines tactics. (It is believed that in a conflict with NATO, SPETSNAZ units would be deployed behind the lines where they would engage in such "active measures" as assassination, kidnapping, bombings, and other terrorist activities.)[15]

Era of Terrorism to Continue

We may make the following concluding comments:

o   Terrorism is growing as a struggle-for-power process, and as a form of surrogate warfare, whereby small groups with direct and indirect state support are able to conduct political warfare at the national level, and ultimately may even succeed in altering the balance of power on the international level.

o   Although predictions are hazardous, it is safe to assume that terrorism, particularly "state-sponsored terrorism," is now an established mode of conflict. It will continue to persist through the 1980s and 1990s because many of the causes which motivate terrorists will remain unresolved, and new ideological and political confrontations will emerge within and among nations. It can be assumed that U.S. adversaries will continue to utilize terrorism -- "warfare on the cheap" -- as a significant tool of their foreign policy.

o   It is an established fact that terrorist groups in Europe, with the direct and indirect support of the Soviet Union, are becoming increasingly potent. Since the lip service paid to detente and peaceful coexistence has not been accompanied by any manifest weakening of the Soviet ambition to achieve regional and global hegemony, the exploitation of terrorism as a tactical tool to disturb the status quo calls for a realistic Western response.

o   The United States and its Free World allies must be prepared to have recourse to a full range of countermeasures. High quality intelligence operations and research are the basic and indispensable ingredients of policies and programs to prevent "state-sponsored terrorism" from destabilizing democratic institutions.

o   Other countermeasures should include clandestine
        counter-terrorist infiltration of terrorist organizations;
        covert U.S. support for foreign counter-terrorist military
        operations; and, selected overt U.S. operations (including
        preemptive attacks) against identified terrorist bases.

o   The United States and its allies need a coherent and firm
        policy for responding to "state-sponsored terrorism."
        This policy should be framed in such a way as to garner
        public understanding and support. It is crucial to move
        vigorously in this direction in order to reduce gradually
        the emerging strategic threat to free democratic
        societies inherent in "state-sponsored terrorism."

NOTES

1. See Lawrence B. Sulc, <u>Active Measures: Quiet War and Two Socialist Revolutions</u> (Washington, D.C.: Nathan Hale Institute, 1984).

2. Ray S. Cline and Yonah Alexander, <u>State-Sponsored Terrorism</u> (Report prepared for the U.S. Army, unclassified, May 30, 1985) p. 39.

3. <u>Ibid.</u> See also Yonah Alexander and Kenneth A. Myers, eds., <u>Terrorism in Europe</u> (New York: St. Martin's Press, 1982); Ray S. Cline and Yonah Alexander, <u>Terrorism: The Soviet Connection</u> (New York: Crane Russak, 1984); Robert H. Kupperman and Darrell Trent, <u>Terrorism: Threat, Reality, Response</u> (Stanford: Hoover Institution Press, 1979); Stefan T. Possony and Francis Bouchey, <u>International Terrorism -- the Communist Connection</u> (Washington, D.C.: American Council for Freedom, 1978); and, Walter Laqueur, <u>Terrorism</u> (Boston: Little, Brown and Co., 1977).

4. "The International Scientific Conference on Terrorism" (Berlin)," <u>Terrorism: An International Journal</u>, Vol. 3, nos. 3 and 4 (1980).

5. For details see, e.g., Alexander and Myers, <u>op. cit.</u>: Laqueur, <u>op. cit.</u>; and Raymond R. Corrado, "Ethnic and Ideological Terrorism in Western Europe," in Michael Stohl, ed., <u>The Politics of Terrorism</u>, 2nd ed., rev. and expanded (New York: Marcel Dakker, 1984), pp. 225-326.

6. For details on various terrorist movements see, e.g., Cline and Alexander, <u>State-Sponsored Terrorism</u>, <u>op. cit.</u>, pp. 135-175.

7. Discussion with U.S. Department of State officials. See also, U.S. Department of State, Bureau of Intelligence and Research, <u>Intelligence Brief</u> (unclassified), December 21, 1984. See also U.S. Department of State, Bureau of Public Affairs, <u>Combatting International Terrorism</u> (March 5, 1985).

8. <u>New York Times</u>, September 16, 1981.

9. <u>New York Times</u>, January 30, 1981.

10. Brian M. Jenkins, <u>Combatting International Terrorism -- The Role of Congress</u> (Santa Monica, California: Rand Corporation, 1977).

11. Karl Marx, <u>Das Kapital</u> (Berlin: Dietz Verlag, 1962), p. 779; and, V.I. Lenin, "Partisan Warfare," in <u>Modern Guerrilla Warfare</u>, ed., F.M. Osanka (New York: Free Press of Glencoe, 1966), p. 68. See also V.I. Lenin, "Left-Wing Communism and Infantile Disorder" in <u>Selected Works</u> (Moscow: Progress Publishers, 1975), pp. 3:301.

12. U.S. Congress, Senate, Committee on the Judiciary, Subcommittee on Security and Terrorism, <u>Historical Antecedents of Soviet Terrorism</u>, Hearings, June 11-12, 1981, 97th Congress, 1st Sess.

(Washington, D.C.: GPO, 1981).

13.   See Nathan M. Adams, "Drugs for Guns," Readers Digest (November 1983), p. 88; Paul B. Henze The Plot to Kill the Pope (New York: Charles Scribner's Son's, 1983); and, Claire Sterling, Time of the Assassins (New York: Holt, Rinehart & Winston, 1984).

14.   See, e.g., Cline and Alexander, Terrorism: The Soviet Connection, op. cit.; John Barron, KGB: The Secret Work of Soviet Secret Agents (New York: Bantam Books, 1974), pp. 76-77; Christopher Dobson and Ronald Payne, The Terrorists: Their Weapons, Leaders and Tactics (New York: Facts on File, 1979); and, Annual of Power and Conflict 1973-1974 (London: Institute for the Study of Conflict, 1974), pp. 230-258.

15.   FPI News Service, January 31, 1985.

Chapter 8

GLOBAL CORRELATION OF FORCES

Roger E. Kanet and Daniel R. Kempton

One of the centerpieces of Soviet international relations theory is the doctrine of the correlation of forces, which refers to the military, economic, political, moral, and other factors that determine the course of history. In Marxist-Leninist thought, history consists of the playing out of the contradictions which exist in the world. During the current stage of history, the central contradiction, or conflict, is that between the socialist camp, led by the Soviet Union, and the capitalist camp, dominated by the United States. The correlation of forces, however, is not restricted to the intrinsic attributes of the two camps. For example, international movements and multinational corporations are also seen as actors which play critical roles within the correlation of forces. For Soviet theorists it is the correlation of forces which determines the outcome of all struggles, in times of both peace and war.[1]

The correlation of forces refers to the struggle of classes in individual countries and in the international arena.[2] Technically, Soviet theorists have never developed a theory of international relations per se, for they do not acknowledge the legitimate, lasting existence of the state.[3] But, for all practical purposes, the correlation of forces can be seen as a Soviet equivalent of a theory of international relations. According to Sanakoyev, a high-ranking Soviet political analyst, the real strength of the Soviet Union is derived from its leadership's understanding of Marxism-Leninism and, thus, the historical class struggle that is currently unfolding.[4]

There has been a tendency among Americans to see the Soviet threat strictly in military terms. U.S. policy -- from the strategy of containment to the Reagan policy of rearmament and peace through strength -- has been based primarily on a concern for military preparedness to respond to possible Soviet aggression. However, Soviet leaders and analysts are quite explicit in noting the role that non-military factors play in the historical struggle between the two world systems. In the words of Sanakoyev:

Speaking of the correlation of forces in the world, we refer, above all, to the correlation of the "class" forces and the struggle of classes both in individual countries and on the international arena, taking into account the real forces -- economic, political, moral and others -- which stand behind these classes. Defining the real forces in international relations, bourgeois scientists as a rule concentrate attention on military and economic factors.[5]

Soviet analysts commonly identify three historic shifts within the correlation of forces. The first shift occurred in 1917 with the creation of the world's first communist state. The second was marked by the defeat of fascism in 1945 and the spread of communism to East Europe and Asia in the ensuing years. The third and most recent modification occurred at the beginning of the 1970s with the USSR's attainment of strategic parity with the United States.

In the view of Soviet analysts, parity forced the United States to abandon its concentration on military force and to enter into strategic negotiations with the Soviet Union, thus ushering in the era of detente. It is important to note that military, rather than economic or political, factors play the critical role in all three events identified by Moscow as major shifts in the correlation of forces.[6]

In the Soviet view, military power is a major, but not preeminent, determinant of the correlation of forces and one in which the USSR excels. Thus, the Soviet buildup changes the correlation of forces. As Deane explains, "Communism can attain its 'inevitable victory' even without war, because the correlation of forces is shifting in its favor."[7]

A major weakness of the doctrine of the correlation of forces stems from the fact that it tends to recognize only uni-directional shifts in force. It cannot recognize or subsequently explain the setbacks and failures of communism -- except by arguing that earlier assessments concerning the state of the balance were incorrect. Although setbacks are often discussed and analyzed in great detail in Soviet literature, this discussion usually occurs outside the context of the theory of the correlation of forces.

Obviously the doctrine is useless in the analysis of a number of major international events. For example, how can one adequately explain the Sino-Soviet split without acknowledging a major setback for the socialist camp? It seems, therefore, that the ideological components of the correlation-of-forces doctrine would significantly impair its utility as an analytical tool.

How Soviet analysts actually calculate the correlation of forces is unclear. In one formulation by Shakhazarov, there are four major components of the correlation -- economic, military, and political factors and international movements[8] -- and the relative importance of these components seems to vary over time. Obviously, the total assessment can be only a rough approximation. As Deane argues, "the global correlation seems to constitute an intuitive calculation of forces based on the Soviet leadership's feel for the direction of world events."[9]

Certainly this type of assessment does not automatically translate into particular foreign policy strategies. However, a clear understanding of the global correlation of forces would provide the Soviet leadership with a heightened awareness of areas of Soviet weaknesses vis-a-vis the West. Unlike their American counterparts, Soviet leaders have not suddenly discovered gaps in their forces, which later turned out to be illusory. Instead Soviet leaders have generally focused on the long-term strengthening of areas of relative Soviet weakness.

Also, since the correlation of forces is seen as the determinant of the outcome of international struggle in times of peace, as well as during war, detente for the Soviet Union did not entail a lessened need to rectify Soviet weaknesses in relationship to the United States. Detente did not imply an end to struggle, but rather a new form of struggle.

Because war between the two camps is no longer viewed as inevitable, military factors do not play an independent role, but they must be viewed as merely a part of the larger correlation of forces. The Soviet military buildup changes the correlation which, in turn, affects world events. Therefore, victories can be won without the use of force, although the availability of military power is critical to those victories.[10]

Historically, the Soviet theoreticians have made use of the correlation of forces on two levels: global and regional.[11] It is used in a global sense to assess the general struggle between the socialist and capitalist camps. It is on this level that we have so far discussed the doctrine.

However, the doctrine is also used to analyze events in a particular region of the world or in a particular struggle. This narrower level is the basis on which the correlation of forces will be examined in the remainder of this paper, with particular reference to the United States and West Europe.

To a very substantial degree Soviet policy toward the countries of West Europe can be viewed as a function of the Soviet-American relationship. Throughout the past three decades, the Soviet leaders have measured their relations with countries such as France and the Federal Republic of Germany in large part by the degree to which those countries pursue policies congruent with or different from the policies of the United States. This is not to argue that other factors, specifically bilateral relations with West Europe, do not play a role in influencing Soviet policy. It means, rather, that Moscow views West Europe as an integral part of the capitalist alliance system which is headed by the United States and, thus, as an extremely important component of the forces arrayed against the USSR.

Europe, both East and West, has remained, over the course of the four decades since the end of World War II, the world region of greatest significance for Soviet military security interests. It is in East Europe that the Kremlin leaders have succeeded in extending most completely their own domination; while in West Europe they face the major concentration of U.S. and allied military power.

Although the specifics of Soviet strategy toward West Europe have been modified over time, several long-term goals have remained constant. The first of these concerns the continuing USSR effort to strengthen its own military position in relationship to the Western alliance system. Attempts to accomplish this goal range from renovating and expanding the military capabilities of the Warsaw Pact, to political-propaganda campaigns aimed at dividing members of the NATO alliance or at preventing the expansion of NATO's military capabilities.

A second, and closely related, Soviet goal in Europe concerns Soviet opposition to the strengthening of West European integration. Although reality has forced the USSR in recent years to grant de facto recognition to the existence of the European Communities, the Soviet leadership has strongly opposed West European unification, most likely because of a concern that a unified West Europe closely allied with the United States would reduce the possibilities for the Soviet Union to bring pressure to bear against individual countries and to continue to try to take advantage of differences dividing members of the Western alliance.

A third set of Soviet goals concerns East Europe. Until the early 1970s, Moscow devoted substantial efforts to gaining from the West recognition of the status quo in East Europe -- including the postwar territorial boundaries, the existence of communist political systems, and also the predominant Soviet position in the region. With the signing of the Helsinki accords in 1975, these goals were largely achieved. However, Moscow is still concerned with the attraction that the West has for the populations of East Europe. As a result, Soviet leaders fear the possible erosion of their dominance in East Europe.

The Military Dimension of Soviet Strategy in Europe

Over the course of the past three decades the Soviet Union and its Warsaw Pact allies have continued to expand and modernize their military capabilities so that by the middle of the 1980s there is no doubt that the Warsaw Pact enjoys significant military superiority in the area of conventional weapons and superiority in theater nuclear weapons as well. The expansion and modernization of conventional weaponry within the Warsaw Pact occurred largely independent of developments within NATO, for no comparable modernization drive occurred in the West during the 1970s.

In addition to the significant increase in conventional armaments available to the Warsaw Pact by the 1980s, the USSR also introduced an entire new generation of intermediate-range ballistic missiles (IRBMs), beginning in the mid-1970s. The SS-20 mobile multi-warhead IRBM provides significant improvements in survivability range, accuracy, and number of warheads in comparison with the SS-4 and SS-5 missiles that they have supplemented or replaced. The Soviet decision to deploy these new intermediate-range missiles has, in effect, resulted in a major shift in relative nuclear capabilities within the European theater. By 1985, for example, the Warsaw Pact possessed approximately 5,700 TNF (tactical nuclear forces) delivery vehicles (with about 8,000 warheads), in comparison with 2,600 NATO delivery vehicles (and 5,500 nuclear warheads).[12]

Closely associated with the actual buildup of Soviet military power in Europe have been the various campaigns mounted by the Soviet leadership to forestall the modernization of NATO military capabilities. At the time that the United States in the late 1970s was considering the introduction of the B-1 bomber and the neutron bomb, for example, Moscow mounted major propaganda campaigns targeted in large part on the citizens of West Europe and the United States. Although there is virtually no evidence to support the argument that Moscow was instrumental in the creation of various peace movements active in the West, Moscow clearly has been interested in supporting these movements and in providing them with verbal ammunition.[13]

After the 1979 NATO decision to deploy cruise and Pershing II missiles in response to the earlier Soviet deployment of SS-20s, Brezhnev and other Soviet leaders made clear efforts to divide the members of the Western alliance on the entire issue of security in Europe and the implications of the NATO missile deployment.[14] They argued that the deployment of U.S. intermediate-range missiles in West Europe represented an attempt by NATO to shift the balance of military capabilities in Europe in favor of the West. Gerhard Wettig has argued that the intransigence of Soviet leaders in the negotiations on INF (Intermediate-Range Nuclear Forces) and the decision to rely heavily on a propaganda campaign against the deployment of the NATO missiles resulted from their assessment of the role that pressure and propaganda had played in bringing about a U.S. decision not to go ahead with the production and deployment of the neutron bomb.[15] However, political conditions in the West were different by the early 1980s -- especially in the United States.

Moreover, despite the ability of opponents of missile deployment to bring out thousands of supporters for demonstrations in West Germany, Great Britain, and even the United States, the decision to go ahead with deployment was never reversed.

Another aspect of Soviet strategy toward Europe has been the attempt to gain U.S. agreement to exclude direct West European security interests from various U.S.-USSR discussions on arms control or limitation. The Soviet insistence, for example, that both French and British nuclear weapons be included in Western calculations of NATO nuclear strength has been aimed, in effect, at ignoring the legitimate separate security interests of West Europe. On the other hand, Soviet leaders have also attempted to convince the Europeans that their security interests diverge from those of the United States, and that Soviet and West European interests overlap and differences between them could be worked out if only West Europe could reduce its dependence on the United States.

Despite the fact that the Soviet Union has managed to establish overall military superiority in Europe, this does not mean that the Soviet leadership is likely to initiate military operations in Europe. First of all, the Warsaw Pact's military advantage is not large enough to ensure military victory, in particular when one takes into account the global military balance between the USSR and the United States. Secondly, the buildup of Soviet military capacities in Europe over the course of the past two decades can be explained, in part at least, by the traditional Soviet approach to security, which emphasizes the ability of the Soviet Union (and earlier Czarist Russia) to match or exceed the military capabilities of all potential opponents simultaneously. However, no matter how one explains the rationale for the recent Soviet military buildup, one factor is quite clear -- the Kremlin has gained a military advantage in Europe.

This advantage has political as well as military implications for the members of the Western alliance system. The USSR has demonstrated in the past that it is well aware of the political advantages that can be gained from the possession of superior military power. Some evidence exists that the growth of Soviet military power has had a degree of influence already on Western policies. In 1975, for example, President Giscard d'Estaing of France stated that West European defense integration should not be pursued because of likely Soviet opposition;[16] moreover, Norway has continued to pursue a policy of unilateral goodwill by excluding military installations from areas close to its border with the Soviet Union.[17] Walter Laqueur has argued strongly that West Europe has already lost the will to defend itself and is on the verge of capitulating to the demands of the USSR.[17]

However, much stronger evidence exists to argue that, despite the extension of Soviet military capabilities in West Europe, the leaders there are not in the process of giving in to Soviet demands.[19] Recent deployment of intermediate-range missiles in West Europe, in the face of strong Soviet pressure, is but the most recent indication that the NATO alliance is not moribund.

The Economic Dimension of Soviet Strategy in Europe

Since at least the beginning of the 1970s economic goals have assumed an importance in Soviet strategy toward West Europe much greater than they had earlier. The moribund state of Soviet technological development and an ingrained fear of running the risks inherent in substantial economic reform and decentralization led the Soviet leaders to pursue an economic strategy based on expanded trade with the West. The purpose of this trade has been, in large part, to gain access to modern technology with which to improve the performance of the Soviet economy. Even though they are now less sanguine about the likely success of this policy, Soviet leaders are still committed to attempts to modernize their economy by importing Western technology. West Europe is, like the United States and Japan, an important source for such technology.

One of the factors that induced the Soviet leaders to pursue a policy of detente during the 1970s was the expectation that improved economic relations would enable them to import Western technology (and to gain the credits necessary to import that technology) as a means of solving some of their long-term economic problems. Although they were successful in obtaining the credits and in importing a much greater array of modern technology, they have since discovered that their economic problems remain.

Furthermore, the Soviet Union in the mid-1980s is still unable to sell much more than natural resources (especially energy), gold, and military equipment on the world market. It has been estimated, for example, that in 1981 these items comprised a full 75 percent of total hard-currency merchandise exports of the Soviet Union, up from about 65 percent in 1977.[20]

Changes in the international political environment since the end of the 1970s have brought with them increased problems for Moscow in expanding trade. The efforts of both the Carter and Reagan administrations to impose sanctions and to strengthen restrictions on trade with the USSR in the wake of the Soviet invasion of Afghanistan and the imposition of martial law in Poland have had a negative impact on the continued growth of Soviet trade with the West. Moreover, the drop in world prices in petroleum over the course of the past several years has cut into the USSR's ability to cover the costs of imports.

In addition to the economic goals that have motivated Soviet commercial relations with the West, foreign trade is also meant to accomplish a number of important political goals. As Angela Stent has noted, Moscow pursues at least three sets of political objectives in its economic relations with West Europe.[21] The primary political objective is to continue to strengthen the West European commitment to detente and, if possible, to induce the Europeans to be more accommodating toward the interests of the USSR -- in return for expanding export markets for West Europe in the USSR. A second probable objective, emphasized by those who oppose the continued expansion of East-West trade, is the creation of Western economic dependence on the USSR -- e.g., in the area of energy -- which the USSR might later be able to use to exert political pressures on West Europe.

A third objective relates to the long-term Soviet interest in dividing the Europeans from their U.S. ally. Since East-West trade has become far more important for the economies of West Europe than it is for the United States, differences in perception have emerged in Europe and the United States concerning the benefits of East-West trade and the rules under which such trade should take place. In recent years, U.S. officials have taken a position that calls for greater restrictions on that trade, particularly with regard to technology with a defense application, while the West Europeans have emphasized the overall benefits that expanded trade with the Soviet Union and East Europe has brought.[22] In the early years of the Reagan administration divisions over East-West trade represented an important source of tension within the Western alliance system.

Although trade with the Soviet Union has become important for most of the major countries in West Europe, in no case does the Soviet Union take more than a small percentage of the exports of a West European country. Moreover, overall West European dependence on the USSR for energy supplies remains modest, particularly among the major NATO countries. By 1990, only 6 percent of the primary energy requirements of France, West Germany, and Italy will be met with Soviet sources.[23]

It must also be kept in mind that any Soviet attempt to use economic pressure against Europe would likely result in retaliation. Although Soviet economic dependence on the West is not great enough to permit the West to exert substantial pressures on the USSR, Moscow's allies in East Europe have a greater dependence on the West and are thus more vulnerable.

Given the poor state of the economies of most of the East European states and their substantial dependence on the West for spare parts, semi-processed raw materials, and technology, it is likely that Western economic pressure would result in serious economic deterioration. Since the Soviet Union is already providing substantial subsidies to most of East Europe,[24] the result would be a major increase in the economic drain on the Soviet economy -- unless the Soviet leadership were willing to run the political risks inherent in permitting economic collapse in one or more East European countries.

In sum, despite the fact that the USSR possesses the world's second largest economy, the Soviet leadership has had minimal success in using its economic potential for foreign policy purposes -- in particular in its relations with the industrial states of the West. It is in the economic dimension of the correlation of forces that the USSR is the weakest. At present, there is little indication that the USSR will be able to improve its position significantly in the near future.

Moreover, the USSR faces serious problems as it attempts to pursue goals which, in part at least, appear to be mutually contradictory. As Moscow continues to build up its military capabilities, it is likely to find that security concerns will increase in both the United States and West Europe. These concerns, in turn, will likely make it more difficult for Moscow to continue to pursue policies aimed at expanding commercial relations with the industrialized West.

The Political Dimension of Soviet Strategy in Europe

Actually many of the political goals of Soviet strategy toward West Europe have already been treated in our discussion of the military and economic dimensions of Soviet strategy. These include, most importantly, the attempt to weaken the relationships between West Europe and the United States. A second, extremely significant, political goal of the USSR has been the desire to gain acceptance by the governments of West Europe of its dominant position in East Europe. To a substantial degree this goal was accomplished in the first half of the 1970s with the signing of a series of treaties, culminating in the Helsinki agreements, which provided Western recognition of the postwar boundaries in Central Europe and committed the West, in particular West Germany, not to consider the use of force to change those boundaries.

During the Polish crisis of 1980-1981, one of the major charges leveled by the USSR concerned alleged Western interference in internal Polish affairs. The Soviet Union and its major East European allies were strongly critical of Western monetary and political support for the independent Solidarity trade union movement. They reiterated the point, made most clearly at the time of the Soviet invasion of Czechoslovakia in 1968, that change in the domestic political systems of the communist states of Europe would not be permitted.[25]

More recently, strong Soviet pressure against the government of Erich Honecker of East Germany, that resulted in his canceling a scheduled visit to West Germany in the summer of 1984, indicated that Moscow is still concerned about the extension of West European relations with the smaller states of East Europe and the possibility that such relations would lessen the Soviet dominant position in the region.

In another area Soviet confidence about trends in domestic political developments in West Europe appears to have waned during the course of the past decade. In 1974-1975, after the establishment of democratic rule in Portugal and the rise of the Portuguese Communist Party (PCP) as a powerful force in domestic politics, the USSR attempted to play an active role in influencing the policies of the PCP.[26] Moscow called upon the Portuguese to learn the lessons inherent in the recent overthrow of the government of Salvador Allende in Chile. But with the defeat of the communists in Portugal, Soviet hopes for the likely success of revolutionary change in West Europe appear to have been tempered.

However, the Communist Party of the Soviet Union (CPSU) was already facing a new challenge from West Europe in the evolution of what came to be called "Eurocommunism." Both the Italian and the Spanish communist parties began publicly challenging the CPSU. Throughout the late 1970s and early 1980s they increasingly refused to accept Soviet ideological tutelage, criticized Soviet attempts to dominate East Europe, and refused to accept the Soviet model as the only one appropriate for revolutionary change.[27]

Throughout the Polish crisis, for example, both the Italian and Spanish communist parties blamed the situation on the "pyramidal and totalitarian" political organization of Soviet-style socialism and called for the immediate development of "democracy and participation."[28] By the spring of 1981 the Soviet and Italian parties were engaged in open polemics on the issue of Poland; other West European communist parties joined in support of political reform within the Polish party and warned Moscow against military intervention.[29]

Despite periodic Soviet statements concerning the coming crisis in capitalist societies, it is clear that they do not expect the West European communist parties, or other elements within the political left for that matter, to have a major impact on developments in the near future. Nor, for that matter, can they any longer be sure that left-oriented political movements are likely to perceive the Soviet Union as the model for the future. To a very large extent the Soviet Union has lost the political advantages once thought to reside in the existence of communist parties in the West. As Hannes Adomeit has noted: "The primary challenge of Eurocommunism is that posed to the legitimacy, validity and relevance of Soviet ideology and the Soviet Union."[30] Moscow can no longer consider communist parties in the West as automatic allies or as instruments of its own policy preferences.

Concluding Comments

From the Soviet perspective, the changes in the U.S.-Soviet global correlation of forces over the course of the past three decades have been largely favorable -- at least up until about 1980. By the early 1970s the USSR had achieved its goal of nuclear parity. Although Soviet nuclear forces today may be technologically inferior to those of the United States, the USSR has more missiles and megatons of destructive capacity than does the United States. In the area of conventional weapons, the Soviet Union continues to maintain a substantial lead, in particular in Europe. Political-psychological factors appear to continue to favor the Soviet Union.

However, the Soviet position vis-a-vis the United States is far from secure. The Soviet economic system is crippled with serious deficiencies, and increases in productivity lag farther and farther behind those of the United States and Japan. Moreover, recent shifts in attitudes within the United States have resulted in a substantial buildup in commitment to refurbishing U.S. military capabilities. As Soviet leaders and political commentators have noted since approximately 1980, the Reagan administration has committed itself to reversing the military trends of the past two decades or so. From the Soviet perspective this represents a direct challenge to the one area within the correlation of forces in which the Soviets have made the most significant gains. Although no authoritative statements have appeared that refer to the possibility of a reversal of the international trend in the correlation, such a possibility is clearly implied in many Soviet writings.[31]

In Europe, as in virtually all other areas of the world, the USSR finds itself in the position of what Paul Dibb has referred to as an "incomplete superpower," which can rely only on military capabilities in an attempt to achieve important foreign policy and security goals.[32]

It must be deeply disconcerting to the Kremlin leaders that NATO has responded to the Soviet military challenge with the deployment of a new generation of nuclear weapons. NATO appears to be involved in a process of renewal; France under the socialist government of Francois Mitterand cooperated with NATO more fully than at any time during the past twenty years.

These NATO-related developments, however, certainly do not mean that the USSR no longer represents a serious challenge to Western interests. The growth of Soviet military power in Europe and worldwide and the likelihood of an extended armaments race between the two superpowers do not present an environment that is conducive to peace and security, either in Europe or on a global scale. The members of the Western alliance must continue to cooperate to develop an integrated approach to their relations with the Soviet Union -- including in the military, the economic, and

102

political realms. If such cooperation can be established, and general long-term Western interests, rather than short-term gains for individual countries, can become the basis for the foreign policies of the Western states, then what the Soviet leaders view as the inexorable change in the international balance in their favor can be reversed. Such a development might help to induce a future Soviet leadership to recognize that the state interests of the USSR will be better served by joining the international community of nations as an important actor and attempting to resolve its differences peacefully, rather than by continuing to be committed to radical change and the dissolution of the current international system.

The authors wish to express their appreciation for comments on an earlier draft of this paper, in particular those of Dr. Hannes Adomeit, Dr. Renata Fritsch-Bournazel, and Dr. Geoffrey Till.

NOTES

1.   Sh. Sanakoyev, "The World Today: Problem of the Correlation of Forces," International Affairs, (1974), No. 11, pp. 40-50. For a brief discussion of the concept of "correlation of forces," see Karen Dawisha, "Soviet Ideology and Western Europe," in Edwina Moreton and Gerald Segal, eds., Soviet Strategy Toward Western Europe. (London-Boston: George Allen & Unwin, 1984), pp. 26-35.
2.   Sanakoyev, "The World Today," p. 42.
3.   R.   Judson   Mitchell,   Ideology   of   a   Superpower: Contemporary   Soviet   Doctrine   on   International   Relations. (Stanford: Hoover Institution Press, 1982), pp. 10-11.
4.   Sanakoyev, "The World Today," pp. 41-42.
5.   Ibid., p. 42.
6.   Michael J. Deane, "The Correlation of World Forces," Orbis, XX (1976), pp. 629-630.
7.   Deane, "Correlation of World Forces," p. 626.
8.   G. Shaknazarov, "K probleme sootnosheniia sil v more," (On the Problem of the Correlation of Forces), Kommunist, no. 3, (February 1974), p. 86.
9.   Ibid., p. 626-628.
10.   Robert   Legvold,   "Military   Power   in   International Politics: Soviet Doctrine on Its Centrality and Instrumentality," in Uwe Nerlich, ed., Soviet Power and Western Negotiating Policies, Vol. 1: The Soviet Asset: Military Power in the Competition Over Europe. (Cambridge, MA; Ballinger Publishing, 1983), pp. 129-130.
11.   Deane, "Correlation of World Forces," p. 627.
12.   Phillip A. Karber, "To Lose an Arms Race: The Competition in Conventional Forces Deployed in Central Europe 1965-1980," in Nerlich, ed., Soviet Power, Vol. I, p. 94; and, NATO and the Warsaw Pact: Force Comparisons (Brussels: NATO Information Service, 1984), p. 7ff.
13.   See Pravda, August 14, 1981, on the U.S. decision concerning the neutron bomb.   For recent Soviet coverage of Western peace demonstrations see, for example, "To Live Next to Pershings?" and "Give Peace a Chance!" New Times, (December 1983), no. 51, pp. 8,9.
14.   See, for example, Brezhnev's interview with West German journalists, Pravda, November 3, 1981.
15.   Gerhard Wettig, "East-West Security Relations at the Eurostrategic Level," in Roger E. Kanet, ed., Soviet Foreign Policy and East-West Relations (New York: Pergamon, 1982), p. 69.
16.   President Giscard d'Estaing at a press conference on May 21, 1975. For an earlier similar statement see Le Monde, May 10, 1974.   Both citations were taken from Hannes Adomeit, The Soviet Union   and   Western   Europe: Perceptions,   Policies,   Problems, National Security series, No. 3/79 (Kingston, Ont.:   Centre for

International Relations, Queen's University, 1979), p. 166.

17. See Seymour Topping, "Under the Shadow of the Kremlin," The New York Times, December 3, 1978.

18. See, for example, Walter Laqueur, "Hollanditis: A New Stage in European Neutralism," in America, Europe, and the Soviet Union: Selected Essays (New Brunswick, NJ-London: Transaction Books, 1983), pp. 33-48.

19. For a discussion of this point see Adomeit, The Soviet Union and Western Europe, p. 165ff.

20. Joan Parpart Zoeter, "USSR Hard Currency Trade and Payments," in U.S. Congress, Joint Economic Committee, Soviet Economy in the 1980's: Problems and Prospects (Washington: U.S. Government Printing Office, 1983).

21. The discussion of this point is based on Angela Stent, "Economic Strategy," in Moreton and Segal, eds., Soviet Strategy Toward Western Europe, pp. 219-220.

22. John P. Hardt and Kate S. Tomlinson, "Soviet Economic Policies in Western Europe," in Herbert J. Ellison, ed., Soviet Policy in Western Europe: Implications for the Atlantic Alliance (Seattle-London: University of Washington Press, 1983), p. 188.

23. Petroleum Economist, Vol. L, no. 2 (1983), p. 51.

24. See Michael Marrese and Jan Vanous, Soviet Subsidization of Trade with Eastern Europe: A Soviet Perspective (Berkeley, CA: Institute of International Studies, University of California, Berkeley, 1983), esp. pp. 145-149.

25. For a discussion of Soviet reactions to developments in Poland see Roger E. Kanet, "The Polish Crisis and Poland's 'Allies': The Soviet and East European Response to Events in Poland," in Jack Bielasiak and Maurice D. Simon, eds., Polish Politics: Edge of the Abyss (New York: Praeger, 1984), pp. 317-344.

26. Joan Barth Urban, "Contemporary Soviet Perspectives on Revolution in the West," Orbis, XIX (1976), p. 1366.

27. For a comprehensive discussion of Soviet relations with West European Communist parties see Joan Barth Urban, "The West European Communist Challenge to Soviet Foreign Policy," in Roger E. Kanet, ed., Soviet Foreign Policy in the 1980s (New York: Praeger, 1982), pp. 171-193.

28. L'Unita, August 19, 1980; cited in Urban, "The West European Communist Challenge," p. 179.

29. See Kevin Devlin, "Soviet-PCI Polemics over Poland," Radio Free Europe Research, RAD Background Report/185 (World Communist Movement), June 30, 1981.

30. Adomeit, The Soviet Union and Western Europe, p. 121.

31. See, for example, the statement by Marshal D.I. Ustinov, Pravda, July 25, 1981.

32. Paul Dibb, The Limits to Soviet Power (London: Macmillan Publishers), forthcoming.

Chapter 9

SOUTHERN FLANK OF NATO

James Arnold Miller

General Umberto Cappuzo, while Chief of Staff, Italian Army, provided a useful overview on the strategic significance of the Mediterranean region:

> The Mediterranean is undoubtedly the most dangerous area, as far as the application of the new forms of Soviet combined strategy is concerned. The only stable thing in the Mediterranean today is instability! And it is here that the dichotomy between freedom and stability, pluralism and order is most apparent. It is a dichotomy which has been present throughout history and which is far from being solved today.

> The Mediterranean is at the crossroads of three continents and three monotheist religions. It is an area of conflict between political, military, ideological, religious and economic blocs. It is a region where more than 300 million people live and as much as 18 different nationalities are present. The absence of a unifying power has its origin in a combination of factors, among which we can mention the mosaic of ethnic national settlements and the strong spirit of autonomy people have developed as a result also of the natural choke points existing in the region. These conditions are also linked to the geostrategic patterns of the area which is characterized by numerous high ridges and passes and narrow seas: that is to say, positions from which the lines of communication can be controlled.

> Sea traffic is very heavy in the Mediterranean: more than 2,000 ocean-going ships are present in the area every day and approximately 40 percent of the energy supplies for Central Europe pass through this basin. This will give some idea of the economic value of the area for the world. The

Mediterranean, however, has not only maintained its role as a vehicle for exchanges of goods and services. It now plays several others. The industrialization of fishing activities, the exploitation of the continental shelf, the use of biological resources: these are all factors that affect international competitiveness and therefore security in the area.

The Arab-Israeli conflict, the Iran-Iraq war, the dispute between Greece and Turkey, the question of Cyprus, the aggressive and dangerous politics of Qadhafi, the Polisario problem referring to the guerrilla group fighting for independence in Western Sahara, the instability of Malta, the revitalization of Islam: these are only some examples of the reasons of conflict. But that is not all! Other crises and hotbeds of tension, even if located outside the Mediterranean, could also have serious repercussions for the area. Events in Afghanistan, in the Persian Gulf, and in the area of the Horn of Africa, examined in a single light, can be grouped together under one threat: the threat to the oil routes to Europe.

To sum up, then, the fulcrum of the East-West confrontation has moved towards the Mediterranean, which therefore becomes the meeting point of three different axes of conflict: East-West, North-South, and South-South. It is around these that the fate of mankind revolves.[1]

The European members of the North Atlantic Treaty Organization on NATO's southern flank include Italy, Greece, Turkey, Spain, and Portugal. Isolated geographically from one another, they do not have a common land front and must depend on sea and air power for their collective security.

Soviet strategy, therefore, against this flank entails the use of substantial naval and air forces to control the Mediterranean area militarily. The Defense Department's publication, Soviet Military Power--1985, pointed out:

The Soviets maintain some 45 ships and submarines in the Mediterranean Sea, where they serve to promote Soviet policies and increase the range of Soviet political and military options in crisis. This contingent of ships, the Soviet Mediterranean Squadron (SOVMEDRON), can be augmented quickly and substantially by units of the Black Sea Fleet. SOVMEDRON units regularly carry out antisurface ship, antisubmarine, and air defense exercises and have participated in joint exercises with Syrian and Libyan forces, as well as with other navies of the Warsaw Pact. SOVMEDRON combatants routinely shadow ships of the NATO nations and have established operating areas near chokepoints. They are thus poised to move quickly to block strategic straits essential to support the Southern Region of NATO . . . .

The Mediterranean and the Middle East have historically been the most active regions of the Third World for Soviet military forces. The Mediterranean Squadron, which includes cruisers, frigates, destroyers, attack submarines, intelligence collection ships, and auxiliaries, is one of the largest, most capable Soviet naval forces operating beyond the USSR's home waters. During peacetime, the Squadron spends time on the surveillance of Western naval forces. The Squadron also supports Soviet interests by its influence-exerting presence on the nations of the Mediterranean littoral and its military support for client countries. Access to ports in the region such as Tartus, Syria, allows the squadron to deploy for extended periods without returning to home waters for maintenance and repair.

Soviet advisory personnel provide a ready capability to aid a client state during a crisis -- aid ranging from increased participation in the operation of sophisticated equipment for the client state's armed forces to covert participation in combat operations. For example, Soviet advisory personnel in Syria are being used to improve the overall effectiveness of the Syrian Armed Forces. The SA-5 surface-to-air missile equipment in Syria, in addition to enhancing Syria's air defense, provides a dramatic symbol of Soviet support. The potential stationing of Soviet troops in Syria, while of questionable military utility, would send a strong political message to both Syria and its potential foes. In the event of war, the Mediterranean Squadron would be tasked with gaining sea control of the eastern Mediterranean and protecting the Soviet Union's southwestern flank. Soviet pilots serving as advisers in Syria, and to a lesser extent in Libya, could be used to fly reconnaissance or combat missions in the region.[2]

Since World War II, the USSR had tried to seize northern Iran; supported insurrection in Greece; attempted to seize control of the Bosphorus and Dardanelles from Turkey; laid claim to Turkish Thrace, the western shore to the Bosphorus, the Dodecanese Islands, Eritrea, Libya, and Malta; and it has made clients at various times and to varying degrees of Yugoslavia, South Yemen, Syria, Iraq, Egypt, Libya, Somalia, and Ethiopia. As in the application of Soviet strategy in other areas of the world, Soviet activities in the Mediterranean have been based on a great deal of opportunism.

However, the record suggests that Soviet strategy toward NATO's southern flank has a number of specific goals, listed in order of increasing relevance to NATO itself: [3]

 o <u>To promote the dynamic status quo</u>. Since Soviet leaders see the <u>status quo</u> to be dynamic, they see it proper and indeed necessary to promote the emergence of socialism and people's democracies. Thus they employ Soviet political, economic, and military resources to support so-called "wars of national liberation," class struggle, and civil strife throughout the Mediterranean region.

 o <u>Limit U.S. influence in the Arab world</u>. Moscow is interested in the location, resources, and religious culture of the Arab states. Although the postwar reduction of British and French power in the Mediterranean, North Africa, and the Middle East has provided opportunities for the expansion of Soviet influence, the United States presence in the area continues as a strategic threat to the southwestern portion of the USSR. Middle Eastern oil also plays an important role in Soviet policies toward the region. Further, with its 37 million Turkic peoples and six million more of the Moslem faith in the Central Asian republics, the USSR is very sensitive to great power involvement in politics of the Arab nations.

 o <u>Limit the value of usefulness of the U.S. tie to Israel</u>. While this objective is related to the previous one, Moscow's efforts to manipulate the Arab-Israeli conflict also are designed to offset the military and strategic advantages which they see accruing to Washington from U.S. cooperation with Israel. Soviet planners no doubt see Israeli bases and facilities of potentially extreme importance to the United States in the event of any conflict in the Eastern Mediterranean, the Middle East, or Southwest Asia.

 o <u>Retain access to Middle East oil</u>. While there is considerable debate among Western observers over the extent to which the Soviet Union will or will not need Middle Eastern oil in the future, it is clear that the USSR's presence in the region -- particularly in Afghanistan, Syria, South Yemen, Ethiopia, and Libya -- gives Moscow a significant option to cut off or at least to disrupt the flow to the West of Middle Eastern oil.

o   <u>Deny to the United States any support from its NATO allies in coping with problems in North Africa, the Middle East, Southwest Asia, and the Persian Gulf</u>. The globally-deployed military and naval forces of the United States pose a threat to the Soviet Union proper and serve to impede Moscow's efforts to expand Soviet influence around the Eurasian periphery and in the Third World. Thus Soviet global strategy aims to make unavailable the bases and facilities from which U.S. forces must operate in forward areas in any conflict. This is especially important in the Eastern Mediterranean. Thus Moscow does all it can to discourage nations in the area from granting or renewing U.S. access to bases, anchorages, and landing and overflight rights.

o   <u>Make NATO politically and militarily incapable of concerted action in crisis and war</u>. Moscow seeks to avoid war and to make it less likely. This is done in part through maintaining the readiness of Soviet military forces to win if engaged and in part through political efforts to deprive NATO of consensus on perceptions of Soviet threats, to stress the differences in the interests of the United States and those of all other NATO members, and to create doubts about American military power and political reliability.

William R. Kintner also has commented on the USSR's combined political and military strategy toward the Mediterranean region. He noted that regional denial is at the heart of this strategy, i.e., Moscow seeks to prevent Western access to regional resources, shipping lanes, and military bases:

    This strategy combines removal of anti-Soviet regimes through destabilization or diplomatic courtship, disruption of Western naval and air links, maintenance of pro-Soviet regimes through arms transfers, and deployment of military posture guaranteeing Soviet input into regional political developments. These policies are interwoven with and mutually reinforcing to simultaneous pursuit of several objectives. Destabilization is furthered by manipulation of political instability. Given the fractured political climate of the Mediterranean Basin, instability can be an instrument for exacerbating political frustration or tension to promote radicalism. This radicalism could threaten Western interests by either removing Western access to the region or constraining the diplomatic options available to politically moderate regimes.

The success of these objectives is dependent on Soviet ability to maintain a prolonged political and military presence in the area. Thus the Soviets have made a sustained effort to remove the vulnerability of their fleet to Western interdiction through Turkey. While Soviet access to bases in Algeria or Syria are essential, they cannot substitute for its Black Sea position. A secure naval passage to the Mediterranean is the essential underpinning of Soviet political influence in this region.[4]

The Four Weak Links in NATO's Southern Flank

The major players on the European stage are Great Britain, France, and the Federal Republic of Germany and are on NATO's northern flank. Italy plays an important role in terms of NATO's central as well as its southern flank. The other four nations on the southern flank are important relative to their neighbors to the north and west, but their contributions to the defense of West Europe are less conspicuous. In the Mediterranean, to the southeast are Greece and Turkey. To the southwest, bordering on the Atlantic Ocean, are Spain and Portugal.

These four nations share a number of common characteristics. The collective memory of each recalls days of bygone imperial glory. Their more recent histories, however, have been less proud. Their economies are, on the whole, weak and underdeveloped compared to those elsewhere on the Continent. In place of the democratic forms of government that characterize their allies, these countries suffered under a variety of dictatorial, military rulers -- they were the black sheep of the North Atlantic Alliance.[5]

Unfortunately, the full integration of these new democracies into the European family of nations has been difficult, despite their membership in NATO. In part this is due to disputes that each has with other members of NATO.

A major objective of Soviet political strategy against West Europe is to promote the disruption of the solidarity among NATO nations and especially to drive wedges between the United States and specific allies in West Europe. While one certainly cannot attribute all frictions within NATO and between individual European NATO countries and the United States to the workings of Soviet strategy, one must acknowledge that the multifaceted and patient political strategy of Moscow seeks to exploit and exacerbate any and all opportunities to pursue its long-term goal in Europe of improving Soviet influence while reducing U.S. influence.

Greece: An excellent on-going case study of Soviet political strategy at work in Europe involves Greece which is increasingly becoming estranged from the United States and from the other European members of NATO. The present situation in Greece cannot yet be viewed as a success for the purposeful actions of Soviet planners in the Kremlin. The Greek government of Premier Andreas Papandreou certainly has a mind of its own and is not a puppet of Moscow. And yet the great degree of confluence between Moscow and the Papandreou government in terms of ideology, attitudes toward the United States, and various international issues suggests -- regardless of the reasons for this confluence -- that if the present trend continues Soviet influence is going to be enhanced in Greece and, indeed, throughout the Mediterranean area, all at the expense of American influence and of overall NATO strategy.[6]

Mr. Papandreou's ruling Pan-Hellenic Socialist Movement (PASOK) won a decisive victory in the June 2, 1985, election, gaining 161 of the 300 seats in the Parliament after a bitter campaign against the conservative, pro-free-enterprise, and pro-NATO New Democracy Party (led by Constantine Mitsotakis). PASOK gained 45.8 percent of the vote or 161 seats; New Democracy 40.9 percent or 126 seats; the Greek Communist Party 9.89 percent or 12 seats; and the Eurocommunist Party, one seat.

Mr. Papandreou and his party are formally committed to the removal of U.S. installations officially described in the party's platform as exposing Greece "to the danger of annihilation in the event of nuclear war." The question is whether Premier Papandreou means what he says or is somehow prepared to deflate the issue and to try to maintain cordial relations with Washington.

Integral to the bases issue is not only Greece's future as a member of NATO but also NATO's Mediterranean strategy. The United States has some 8,000 military personnel and dependents at four major facilities in Greece: Hellenikon Air Force Base and the Nea Makri Naval Communication Center in Greece proper, and on Crete the Souda Bay naval anchorage and port facilities and the Iraklion air support facility which includes an airfield used for reconnaissance flights and a missile firing range.

The U.S. presence in Greece and Crete includes important early warning sites, a major fleet communications system, ammunition depots, storage facilities, and a major electronic intelligence surveillance station at Iraklion which monitors Soviet activities. In short the bases on Greece/Crete are of great importance to the U.S. Sixth Fleet, to the U.S. Air Force, and to U.S. intelligence gathering. Greece is thus, for Washington, of crucial importance to U.S. interests and to NATO. Moving the base facilities to Sicily and in part to Turkey would not overcome the reality that the United States regards Greece as a vital link between Europe and the Middle East.

Under an agreement signed on September 8, 1983, the United States may use the Greek facilities for five years. The agreement provides that the agreement is terminable after five years upon written notice by either party to be given five months before the termination. Since the agreement also allows the United States seventeen months commencing on the effective date of termination to withdraw U.S. personnel, property, and equipment from Greece, this means that in the worst of circumstances the U.S. presence would have to be terminated toward the end of 1989.

Mr. Papandreou's PASOK gained a four-year term to head the Greek government in the election of October 1981, ending thirty years of conservative governments. Greek political analysts believe he called for early elections because he saw the economy getting worse, or perhaps because he feared that his conservative opponents might use the remaining time to improve their organization and abilities to win a general election. Papandreou, 66, a U.S. Navy veteran, an ex-U.S. citizen, and a former economics professor at the University of California at Berkeley, has promised recently to honor his earlier pledges to close down U.S. bases by 1990 and to lessen Greece's NATO role. While Papandreou signed the 1983 bases agreement, he has since described the pact as an accord to dismantle the bases.

Despite Papandreou's recent stated commitments to remove the American military presence by the time the present agreement expires, some analysts believe that he will not do so. They point to the fear of the Greek government that ending the American military presence will result in building up the strength of traditional arch-rival Turkey and also neutralize the powerful political leverage of the so-called Greek lobby in Washington. A move to end the American use of the bases could also adversely affect Greece's already troubled economy. In return for the bases, the United States provides Greece with $500 million in military aid, mostly aircraft and other materiel needed to modernize the Greek armed forces. Greece's economy is in terrible shape, with inflation running at 18-20 percent, the highest in the European Economic Community, and the jobless rate is 10 percent.

Perhaps Papandreou will strive to walk the tightrope between his commitment to close the bases and his need to benefit from U.S. military aid in exchange for the bases, while at the same time continuing reasonably good relations with the European Economic Community. Despite much friction since his election in 1981, Papandreou has stayed in NATO, and won Common Market subsidies for Greek farmers.

The fact is that relations between Washington and the socialistic and increasingly pro-Moscow Papandreou government are likely to remain strained. Even if America can continue to use the bases, Greece's status as an effective partner in NATO is being eroded. Papandreou has tried to establish solid relations with the Soviet bloc, has supported moves toward a nuclear-free zone in the Balkans, and has repeatedly pledged to end Greece's adherence to one specific bloc. He has also been very friendly with communist leaders and with Libyan leader Mu'ammar al-Qadhafi; he has opposed the deployment of U.S. cruise and PERSHING II missiles in Europe; and, he has boycotted NATO military exercises.

In addition, Papandreou has toed Moscow's line with regard to the shooting down of Korean Airlines Flight 007 in the fall of 1983, and concerning the repression of the Solidarity labor movement and other repressive measures in Poland. The premier is able to take advantage of a strong anti-American feeling in Greece, a sentiment which according to polls by the U.S. Information Agency is deepest among ten European countries surveyed.

Since Papandreou's socialists won a majority of the seats in the Parliament in the June election, they did not have to consider entering into a coalition with the communists. The pro-Moscow Greek Communist Party has made it clear that the price it would demand for support of a minority Socialist government is a commitment to close the bases, leave NATO, and end ties with the European Community. The Greek situation thus provides a tremendous opportunity for the Kremlin to apply pressure.

At this point about all Washington can hope for is that Greece's economic and other domestic problems will cause Papandreou and PASOK to become more "reasonable." Or perhaps Washington can hope that conditions will get so bad in Greece that in the next round of elections -- due in four years -- the conservative forces will be elected. In any case, America's options with regard to Greece seem very limited at the present time.

Turkey: The Reagan administration has been sounding out Turkey about that nation's future role in U.S. global strategic planning in the event that Greece closes the U.S. bases and facilities in Greece. Reportedly President Reagan, Secretary of Defense Caspar Weinberger, and Secretary of State George Shultz discussed this topic with Turkish Prime Minister Turgut Özal during his visit to Washington in early April 1985. It is not thought that Turkey would oppose an increased U.S. military presence. There are already some 5,000 American military personnel serving in that nation. Turkey could be expected to ask for increased military aid, or to request that the United States write off some $3.5 billion of Turkish military debts, in return for an increased U.S. military presence in Turkey. Any new U.S. aid would be in addition to existing levels of military assistance, e.g., for fiscal 1986, the Reagan administration has requested $939 million of assistance to Ankara, of which $785 million is military.[7]

Aside from the issue of the Greek bases, Turkey is strategically important in its own right. It has a 1,500-mile land and

Black Sea border with the Soviet Union, and the second largest NATO land force after America's. The Turkish navy will play a vital role in any conflict with the USSR. Turkey operates the only ingress/egress route between the Mediterranean and Black Seas. The Turks also have the only Free World naval combatant bases on the Black Sea. For Moscow planners, the major threat to either successful reinforcement of Soviet naval forces in the Mediterranean, or to a preemptive withdrawal of these forces into the Black Sea, is the Turkish Straits cork. The Turkish Straits are comprised of the Bosporus and Dardanelles with the Sea of Marmara forming a sort of refuge area between two gauntlet lines. Reportedly the Turkish Navy, while combat-ready and with substantial resources, needs continued modernization and better training to assure that the Black Sea remains a Soviet lake and not the major staging area for Soviet naval combatants to challenge NATO for control of the Mediterranean.[8]

Another problem for American and NATO planners is that nowhere along borders shared with the Warsaw Pact are the odds any worse for NATO. Turkish morale is high, and most Turks are strongly anti-Soviet. But the Turks know that they need aid from the United States to help them fulfill their NATO-assigned task in a future war: To stop the USSR from punching through eastern Turkey and grabbing oil-rich Middle East areas. NATO reports there are twelve modern Soviet divisions stationed along the Turkish border, with eight nearby that could be committed to an assault. To resist them, Turkey could muster eight divisions, equipped mainly with Korean War arms, and could summon four more divisions from southern Turkey. The Turkish forces are heavily outnumbered in tanks and artillery weapons by the Soviet forces. In a war with the USSR, Turkey could count on quick ground reinforcement and air support from NATO allies to help control the Turkish Straits, but in the remote east, its forces likely would have to hold out alone for weeks, backed only by U.S. warplanes stationed in Turkey.[9]

The Soviet Union can be expected to continue to try to exploit Greek-Turkish differences. Moscow will point to any military buildup by Turkey as a threat to Greece. Moscow encourages and reports statements of the Greek government of Andreas Papandreou like the one Mr. Papandreou made while Turkish Prime Minister Özal was in Washington: he said Greece feels no danger from its communist neighbors but feels threatened by Turkey.[10]

Spain and Portugal: The accession of Spain and Portugal to the European Economic Community (EEC) has created major problems between these nations and the EEC nations. Issues include the eligibility of Spain and Portugal for large economic subsidies and grants -- which would strain the resources of the EEC's already troubled budget and reduce funds for poorer member countries like Italy and the Irish Republic. Another problem has been Spain's desire for extensive fishing rights in EEC waters, a desire opposed by other countries, especially France.[11]

A festering sore for NATO is the possibility that Spain might leave NATO -- or at least might diminish further its already limited role within the alliance -- because of domestic politics. Spain's Prime Minister, Felipe Gonzalez, while campaigning for office in 1982, said he would allow a referendum on whether Spain should stay in NATO. He has had to walk a delicate tightrope within his own Socialist Party over the NATO issue. In mid-December 1984 anti-NATO members won 40 percent of the vote on the NATO question at the Socialist Party Congress.[12]

Another problem involving Spain and NATO is Spain's continuing impatience over the British position with regard to Gibraltar. The failure of talks between London and Madrid has led Madrid to threaten to withdraw from NATO if its interests in Gibraltar are not satisfied. Such statements could represent more posturing than serious intent but nonetheless they underscore that Spain and Britain both claim sovereignty over the Rock of Gibraltar. The people of Gibraltar have expressed in a referendum that they wish to remain British.[13]

Despite President Reagan's visit to Spain in May 1985, during which he promised to assess reducing the American military presence there, many analysts believe that the main U.S. bases in Spain are irreplaceable. These bases include Torrejon Air Base, Zaragoza Air Base, and the Rota naval facility. The Rota facility supports the U.S. Sixth Fleet and anti-submarine capabilities in the Mediterranean. Spain is a proposed staging area for NATO's ACE Mobile Force of ground troops to be rushed wherever NATO's southern flank is threatened. The Spanish bases will become even more important for the United States and NATO if Greek Prime Minister Papandreou makes good his threat to cancel American access to important Greek air and naval facilities in 1988.[14]

Portugal's relations with other NATO members are not complicated by an issue as complex as Gibraltar. However, the question of Portuguese membership in the EEC, and various domestic actions by Portugal's socialist-led government, e.g., concerning land reform, have created some difficulties in Lisbon's relations with its allies. Moscow will continue to try to improve its ties with the socialist government in Lisbon, and to try to create wedges in Portuguese relations with the other members of NATO.[15]

NATO and the "Out of Area" Problem

At present, NATO's legal southern boundary is the Tropic of Cancer. NATO strategists are concerned with out-of-area or out-of-region threats to NATO where the formal NATO treaty area could be militarily outflanked and compromised by Soviet-backed Third World contingents in the more peripheral regions.[16]

Sir Patrick Wall, President of the North Atlantic Assembly, was recently asked if he saw any possibility of NATO's boundaries being extended either through an amendment to the NATO Treaty, or at least in practice:

> This is an important question, because the threat to NATO is now worldwide because the Russian threat is worldwide. And, as you say, NATO is bounded by the Tropic of Cancer. There is no question in my view. . . that the treaty could and maybe should be renegotiated, but that is not about to happen anytime soon, if ever. I am afraid the boundaries will remain as they are. But what you can do is use the maritime powers of NATO, as we are doing at the moment -- the Americans, the British, and the French have fleets of ships in the Indian Ocean, which is well outside the treaty area. So to some extent some of the NATO machinery -- communications, etc. -- can be used on an ad hoc basis by the maritime powers of NATO. But anything outside the legal boundaries is not a NATO operation. That must be quite clearly understood.[17]

Sir Patrick lamented that at present the American carrier task force in the Indian Ocean protecting the Strait of Hormuz, the two British destroyers or frigates and a supply ship in the area, and the several French ships permanently based in the Indian Ocean do not work together, at least not officially. He stated that he would like to see something like a combined NATO fleet operating in the area.[18]

Sir Patrick also noted that the complex political and military situation in Southern Africa is of vital importance to NATO even though it is beyond the NATO boundaries. This region is the focus of intense Soviet efforts to support so-called wars of national liberation and radical regimes, to enhance Soviet and proxy military power projection capabilities, and to be in a position to deny/disrupt Western access to not only oil transported around the Cape of Good Hope but also the strategic and critical nonfuel minerals produced in Southern Africa, especially in South Africa.[19]

NOTES

1.   General Umberto Cappuzo, "NATO's Future -- Coping with Challenge," paper presented at the Defense Strategy Forum of the National Strategy Information Center, Washington, D.C., March 6, 1984.

2.   U.S. Department of Defense, Soviet Military Power -- 1985 (Washington, D.C.: Government Printing Office), pp. 106, 118.

3.   These objectives were identified in Thomas H. Etzold, "The Soviet Union in the Mediterranean," Naval War College Review, July-August 1984, pp. 5-10. Most of the accompanying discussion is also drawn from his article.

4.   William R. Kintner, "Soviet Expansion in the Mediterranean Region," Crossroads: An International Socio-Political Journal, no. 13, 1984, pp. 2-3.

5.   Anthony Korenstein, "Two Soft Points Threaten NATO Stability," Defense Systems Review and Military Communications, July/August 1984, p. 32.

6.   The information in the following paragraphs about Greece has been drawn from the following sources: James M. Perry, "Greece's Papandreou Is Reelected in Greece," Washington Post, June 3, 1985, p. A-1; "What Matters to Greece," New York Times, June 4, 1985, p. A-5; Joseph Kraft, "Another Lesson From Greece," Washington Post, June 6, 1985, p. A-27; and Andrew Borowiec, "Papandreou Victory Revives Question of Future U.S. Bases," Washington Times, June 7, 1985, p.   6-A.   For useful background information, see John C.   Loulis, "Greece Under Papandreou: NATO's Ambivalent Partner," European Security Studies no. 3, Institute for European Defence and Strategic Studies (London), 1985; and, Panoyote E.   Dimitras, "Greece: A New Danger," Foreign Policy, no. 58, Spring 1985, pp. 134-150.

7.   Russell Warren Howe and Jeremiah O'Leary, "U.S. Discusses Turkish Role if Greece Withdraws Support," Washington Times, April 2, 1985, p. 6-A.

8.   See Stephen K. Chadwick, "Eastern Anchor of NATO," Proceedings (U.S. Naval Institute), March 1985, pp. 129-132.

9.   "Remote Frontier Where East, West Could Clash," U.S. News and World Report, April 8, 1985, p. 31.

10.   See, "Turkey: Not an East Partner," Washington Post, April 5, 1985.

11.   Korenstein, pp. 32-33.

12.   "Spain and NATO: Felipe Fights Back," The Economist, December 22, 1984, p. 32.

13.   See T. R. Milton, "The Increasing Importance of Spain and Portugal," Air Force Magazine, August 1981, pp. 74-79.

14.   "Spain's Premier Pledges His Nation Will Stay in NATO, U.S. News and World Report, June 2, 1985, p. 2; and Milton. "The

118

Increasing Importance of Spain and Portugal."

15. Korenstein, pp. 33-35; Milton, Op. cit.

16. William T. Tow, "NATO Out-of-Region Challenges and Extended Containment," Orbis, Vol. 28, no. 4, Winter 1985, pp. 835-836.

17. Sir Patrick Wall, "NATO: From North of Norway to South of Simonstown," interview in Sea Power, November 1984, p. 62.

18. Ibid.
19. Ibid., pp. 62-66.

Chapter 10

NORTHERN FLANK OF NATO

Finn Sollie

Northern Perspective

As seen from mainland Europe, the northern flank will easily appear as a mere appendix to the central European defense area, and Soviet strategy in the north will be assessed for its role as part of a large-scale strategy against West Europe. From the North American point of view, emphasis will be put on the even greater scale strategy at the global level and, moreover, special observations will be made in regard to the role and implications of a very real, direct nuclear threat against North America from Soviet bases and adjacent waters in the Kola and Barents Sea area. This particular dimension of the Soviet northern flank strategy may be less immediately apparent to the European observer and carry a different meaning to him than to the American observer. Needless to say, a typical Scandinavian naturally will be concerned primarily with the relevance of Soviet strategy to his own security, and he will read the facts as he sees them, in that particular light.

There is one particular question about Soviet strategy which most Scandinavian observers will feel impelled to ask at one point or another -- and that goes for all Scandinavians and not only for those from states that belong to the North Atlantic Treaty Organization (NATO): Is the Soviet threat against the northern flank merely a part of the wider strategy against NATO, or a threat that exists because Norway and Denmark (and Iceland) have joined NATO? Said another way: Is there, in fact, a separate Soviet threat against the northern countries of Europe which follows a strategy of its own and which will be pursued in any event, either as part of the current larger strategy against NATO or as a strategy of its own, as if NATO were irrelevant?

NATO opponents, of course, will claim that there is no Soviet threat against the northern countries as such, and consequently, that all the Nordic countries would be more safe and secure if none of them were NATO members. Such arguments disregard the fact that in any event geographical location and potential strategic value in an international conflict may attract outside interests and involve risks which neutrality cannot prevent. By blaming a Soviet threat against the northern countries exclusively on the existence of NATO and the Soviet strategy against the alliance, neutralists disregard historical experience, including the fate of Finland, Denmark, and Norway during World War II. They also overlook the fact that the Soviet Union may have special interests of its own in the northern region and will pursue those interests if and when it can and by whatever means it finds feasible.

This also means that to the extent that the Soviet Union does, in fact, have special interests in the northern flank area -- and a strategy for pursuing them -- the NATO northern flank countries are, indeed, faced with special problems in addition to the joint and common problems within NATO. It also means that from the point of view of northern NATO countries, and particularly of Norway, which has a common border with the Soviet Union, it will be necessary to face the question of Soviet northern flank strategy in a perspective which will include special regional interests. Some of those regional Soviet concerns obviously will be reinforced by goals and intentions vis-a-vis NATO, e.g., local maritime security interests which, by the way, are far older than the present East-West division. Other Soviet interests in the area may be more typically local in nature, e.g., in regard to offshore resource rights and legal issues which are essentially non-strategic in nature. Nevertheless, such local and non-military interests also may result in policies and actions which will arouse security concerns as well, and thus become involved in strategic considerations.

Thus, it is not possible to make a sharp and clear distinction between a Soviet strategy against NATO on the northern flank, on the one hand, and a Soviet strategy directed specifically against the Nordic countries, on the other hand. The issues are on the whole closely interwoven and often mutually confusing. Also, issues, interests, and problems in the northern region have evolved rapidly over the last few decades, and this too adds a special dimension to strategic considerations in the region.

Northern Development

The most significant change of a military nature has been the dramatic development since the early 1960s of the Soviet Navy, and particularly of its Northern Fleet which is based in the Murmansk region, not far from the Norwegian border. Regional implications of this development clearly are closely related to the expanding role of Soviet naval power in the Atlantic and, even at the global level, to the special role of newer generation strategic submarines in the deterrent balance between the Soviet Union and the United States.

Another major change is that which follows from the extension of coastal state jurisdiction to include resources (first in 1958) on the continental shelf and (then in 1982) in the waters of extended national exclusive economic zones as well. One result of this has been that Soviet vessels of any kind will have to pass through or operate in waters which are subject to special coastal state jurisdiction. While the new Law of the Sea (which a number of key nations, including the United States, have not yet signed) does not impose restrictions upon naval movements and naval exercises beyond territorial limits or authorize coastal state interference, a new legal regime has nevertheless been drafted whose effects could be important. In any case, such developments have underscored a need to establish border lines between neighboring jurisdictions, and to determine the exact status of special zones where other parties may claim special rights. Both problems have become acute and urgent in those northern waters which are so sensitive in a strategic sense because of the role and importance of the Soviet Navy.

Negotiations between Norway and the Soviet Union on the dividing line in the Barents Sea so far have produced no result. Despite talks for more than ten years, the chances for a solution still seem remote. The disagreement concerns an area which is larger than the whole Norwegian zone in the North Sea (south of 62° northern latitude). This is also a question about the exercise of exclusive jurisdiction to determine who shall be given permission to carry out offshore activities there, including the installation and operation of offshore structures for petroleum development.

In the Svalbard/Spitsbergen area, questions have been raised about the possible application of special stipulations or provisions of the Spitsbergen Treaty of 1920 concerning free access and equal rights for prospecting and development of resources for persons and companies from all the states which are party to the treaty. Here, hundreds of thousands of square kilometers of ocean space are involved (with exact size depending on delimitations). The question is decisive for who will be entitled to operate there, as well as for the rate and location of development. Some forty parties are concerned, including all states which have companies with technical and economic capabilities for offshore petroleum activities.

An additional significant change in northern area development is that of very rapid expansion of resource development and industrialization. One obvious illustration of this is the massive development during the last few decades of hydrocarbon resources in the West Siberian Basin, north of 60° northern latitude. Already, more than 50 percent of Soviet oil production is coming out of this region and more than two thirds of proven Soviet natural gas resources have been found within the Arctic region. Offshore exploration in the Barents Sea also has begun. At its western edge (Tromsoflaket) significant finds of both oil and gas already have been made, and it is only a matter of time before commercial development begins. The Soviet Union has begun exploration in the Barents Sea, so far with two drilling ships working, one at the border of the disputed area which is claimed by both Norway and the USSR, and one much farther to the east. Exploration is also scheduled for the Kara Sea, between Novaya Zemlya and the Yamal Peninsula. Soviet plans now call for twelve rigs to operate in the Barents Sea by 1990, and if oil, rather than natural gas, is found before then, activities will be expanded. As part of this development, an offshore supply base is being built in the Murmansk area, including a half-mile of deep-water docking facilities. At the same time, a new college for petroleum-oriented studies is being established in Murmansk for 1,200 students, and the maritime institute is being updated to train personnel in offshore navigation and operations.

These developments may have significant effects also in a strategic context. One obvious effect is that the role and importance of the northern region will increase quite considerably in economic and industrial terms. In the Soviet Union this will continue the trend which has been remarkable for several decades. Offshore petroleum development in northern Norway may bring rapid economic development to that province. In this connection, it must be remembered that Norway's northern continental shelf (to the north of 70° northern latitude) accounts for more than 50 percent of the total Norwegian shelf area -- how much more depends on the final delimitation vis-a-vis the Soviet Union -- and that much of the northern area appears to be promising for petroleum development. By comparison, the Norwegian part of the North Sea continental shelf, which is the basis for current production, is less than 15 percent of the total Norwegian shelf area (to the 600 meter depth limit).

Development of northern resources obviously will be of primary interest to the northern states themselves. Nevertheless, any massive development of northern petroleum resources also will attract the interest of energy-importing states, particularly in West Europe. Soviet gas deliveries to Europe, which have caused so much debate by raising questions about security of supply as well as of the wisdom of supporting Soviet economic development, do come from the northern fields and must continue to do so if that trade is to be maintained. Together with the Soviet Union, Norway is the only net exporter of oil in Europe, and Norway also has a considerable potential for increased deliveries of natural gas. The rate and speed of Norwegian offshore development in the north will be determined by Norwegian authorities. Market conditions obviously will be important for policy decisions. In any event, northern offshore development potentials and policies will attract very considerable attention over the next few decades, and much of that attention will not only be economic but also political.

International Participation in Northern Development

Extension of coastal state jurisdiction and exclusive sovereign rights to natural resources on the continental shelf and in the waters of the 200-mile exclusive economic zones have the effect of excluding foreign or international participation in the resources development. For centuries, fishing, whaling, and sealing have attracted men and vessels from Europe to the rich fishing grounds off Northern Norway and in the Barents Sea. With the establishment of exclusive economic zones (and also the result of reduced stock) foreign fishing has dropped dramatically in northern waters, although there is still some participation in the Svalbard area, where a non-discriminatory fisheries protection zone has been established, rather than an exclusive national zone. Even there, however, vessels from Great Britain, France, and West Germany which used to come there in great numbers have greatly reduced their participation (while Spanish trawlers have increased their activity). Because there is now very little international shipping in the area, the net effect has been a great reduction of foreign presence in these northern waters. For all practical purposes, Norway and the Soviet Union could soon become the only two countries with regular non-military activities there and the Barents Sea might, in fact, turn into what former Soviet Fisheries Minister Isjkov liked to call the "joint Soviet-Norwegian Sea." That is, this might happen if both countries were to exclude foreign participation in offshore petroleum activities. With foreign participation on the northern continental shelf, however, a constant international interest will be maintained.

The potential strategic importance of northern offshore development may be quite considerable, but should not be overestimated. In view of the Norwegian position, several points nevertheless should be made. First, the existence of a petroleum potential, which attracts international interest, and the participation of international companies in the development on the northern continental shelf may serve as an insurance policy against Soviet pressure for special, bilateral arrangements in the north, possibly designed to secure Soviet influence. The existence of a third party commercial interest and presence may, in given situations, provide significant psychological support. For instance, if the Soviet Union should attempt to harrass operations or to influence Norwegian policy for offshore development in an area where foreign companies are present, that would arouse international interest and concern. Consequently, backing may follow for the Norwegian position vis-a-vis its powerful neighbor. This is not to say that it will be a good idea for Norwegian authorities to solicit outside support to enhance their bargaining position, but rather that the situation itself is developing in a way where firmness may be maintained and undue interference and unnecessary episodes may be more easily avoided.

Secondly, to the extent that the Soviet Union does have a need for foreign technology and know-how to develop its own offshore resources, this will further inspire a sensible policy for maintaining low tension and avoiding controversy in the area. In this context, maintaining good relations with Norway becomes almost a necessity for the Soviet Union, because bad relations will not only jeopardize needed cooperation with Norwegian firms, but may create problems for cooperation with international companies as well. For various practical reasons, foreign companies may find it impractical and difficult to cooperate with the Soviet Union in northern offshore development without some involvement of Norwegian interests and the acquiescence of Norwegian authorities, inter alia, to secure transport, supply, and bases for operations. Furthermore, if companies were to feel that they might have to choose between Soviet contracts and Norwegian goodwill in a period of tension, they might see their best advantage in maintaining their Norwegian contacts. For instance, they cannot help but be aware that Norway's northern continental shelf is larger than the Soviet Barents Sea shelf and, moreover, that the proportion of resources which will be available to the international market may be much greater on the Norwegian than on the Soviet side of the (future) dividing line.

The possibility of offshore petroleum development in the Svalbard region raises a special problem which is of interest to a number of states and where the final outcome may have considerable impact upon the development of offshore activities in this large area of northern waters, and upon the pattern of presence and operations in the northwestern part of the Barents Sea. Here too indirect strategic and security concerns are involved.

Under the terms of the Spitsbergen Treaty of 1920, countries that are parties to the treaty have guaranteed access to the islands for their citizens and companies. They may explore and exploit natural resources in these countries under completely equal treatment. Also, taxation in the islands is lenient and favorable to investors (for instance, tax on production value, which in the North Sea may amount to 85 percent, cannot exceed 1 percent). By the letter of the treaty, these special conditions apply to the islands and their territorial waters (which extend to the four-mile limit, but may be further extended to twelve miles under the new Law of the Sea convention). In the view of the Norwegian government those provisions cannot be interpreted to mean that those rights shall apply to the continental shelf (and the waters) beyond the territorial limit as well. Other governments have reserved their position on the question, or openly protested. The Soviet Union, however, lodged a formal protest at an early date.

At present, only Norway and the Soviet Union have permanent settlements and regular commercial activities at Svalbard, and this has been the basis for constant Soviet claims for a special relationship and for demands for prior consultation before Norway adopts and enforces new regulations and policies. Offshore development under treaty provisions obviously would destroy any base for those demands and solidify international presence and interest in the area.

A Rich but Vulnerable North

In an historical perspective, the rapid surge for development of northern regions is one of the important events of the present age. The Soviet Union in particular is making a massive effort in this respect. Something like one half of the Soviet land territory is Arctic in the sense that it lies in the permafrost zone (continuous and non-continuous). Much of that land can be reached and developed only by maritime transport in the far north, along the coast and up (and down) the rivers. For this reason the Soviet effort to develop Arctic shipping is an essential element of northern resource development.

In a slightly longer perspective, further development and increased numbers of nuclear ice-breakers also will serve to develop transpolar shipping between the North Atlantic and the North Pacific on a permanent, year-around basis. Such developments will not only expand the resource base for economic development in the Soviet Union, but it may also give the Soviet Union a competitive advantage for maritime transport between the Far East and European, as well as American east coast, ports. Together with the container capacity on the Trans-Siberian Railroad and the new BAM line, this may add up to an international capacity which Western countries may want to regard with considerable concern, especially in a long-term strategic context.

Other countries too, are making considerable progress in developing their northern resources, albeit on a somewhat smaller scale and, so far at least, with less emphasis on Arctic navigation and maritime transport than in the Soviet Union. The trend is clear, however, and while the Soviet Union is greatly advanced in nuclear ice-breaker technology, Western countries are more advanced in other fields. The total result of these developments is that now, some 400 years after the first systematic effort to penetrate the Arctic, the northern polar region is finally being opened for all kinds of operations and activities.

Already transpolar air routes have been established, and nuclear submarines cruise the depths of the Arctic Ocean more or less at will, posing a hidden threat which is not easily countered. This is not the place to discuss the implications of the direct nuclear threat across the polar wastes between the two superpowers. But we should point out that just as technology made possible the operations of the U.S. Strategic Air Command, the installation of the ring of air bases and warning installations along the Arctic fringe, and the operation of submarines in the Arctic, technology is now permitting development to the extent that the Arctic Ocean is gradually turning into another world ocean, or into an "Arctic Mediterranean" as foreshadowed by the Canadian Vilhjalmur Stefanson some sixty years ago. Thus, the Soviet Union is also facing the prospect of becoming a true coastal state in the far north, with many of the advantages and disadvantages involved.

The Arctic coast will never have the same quality as a blue-water coast, but new technologies and new activities and maritime operations under Arctic conditions do make northern lands less difficult to approach, if not exactly more easily accessible. To that extent, the several thousand kilometers of Soviet coastline will gradually become more exposed. One may wonder if this will ever prove to be a real problem or not, but the Russian mind appears to have a fixation on the dangers of exposure in the Arctic, and the Soviet government appears overanxious to guard its northern lands against any possible intrusion.

In this context, development and change in the northern border region to Norway and the NATO northern flank will be particularly important. Here, a series of legal and political problems must be solved, and policies established for relations with a neighboring state and with outside parties in the continuing process of Arctic development. The Barents Sea and Svalbard region make an area which is doubly important, for here is the main access route into the Polar Basin and the gateway for navigation and operations deeper in the Arctic Ocean and in its rim sea regions.

Even more important though, is the fact that this is the area where the Soviet Navy has its main exit into international waters, and where strategic interests and national security are most directly exposed to the combined changes which follow from the new Law of the Sea, from offshore resource development, and from the new concentration of international interest in northern area development. By coincidence, these changes are happening at the very time when the Soviet Union is emerging as a true maritime superpower and beginning to learn to use its new sea power as an instrument for promoting Soviet state interests on a global scale, rather than as a coastal defense force to protect the Soviet continental domain against foreign intruders.

The Military Threat

NATO is a defensive alliance whose primary purpose is to deter and, if necessary, to resist and repel any armed attack upon any of its members. NATO thinking about Soviet strategy, therefore, is and must be concerned primarily about the Soviet military threat, and about the plans and capabilities of the Soviet Union (and its allies) to apply its military power offensively against any part of the NATO territory and any NATO forces. Under article 5 of the North Atlantic Treaty, "an armed attack against one or more of (the members of the alliance) in Europe or North America shall be considered an attack against them all" and, consequently, as a result of the commitment to collective defense within NATO, any plan to use armed force against any part of the NATO defense area must be based on the assumption that a local attack will be seen and responded to as an attack upon all. Any strategy against NATO's northern flank therefore must be worked out on the assumption that any attack there will escalate to general war and that the regional battle will have to be fought as part of an overall strategy.

The NATO northern flank in Europe consists of the area under the North European Command, with headquarters at Kolsas (near Oslo) and includes Allied Forces North Norway, Allied Forces South Norway, and Allied Forces Baltic Approaches. In purely geographical terms, these forces will defend a vast area with complex and varied defense problems.

For reference, it should be remembered that the distance from Kirkenes to Kiel, as mainland extremes of the AFNORTH area, is equal to the distance from Bremerhaven to Reggio (at the Strait of Messina), or from Paris to Ankara. Equally important, adjacent to the AFNORTH area lie the vast stretches of northern waters and the islands where defense is part of the responsibility of Allied Command Atlantic, from the Faeroes to the North Pole and from Svalbard to South Greenland, and including Iceland (and for that matter, Jan Mayen) as well.

For East and West alike, the strategic importance of these combined areas which make up the northern flank can hardly be overestimated. It has been said that while it might not be possible for the alliance to win a war in those waters, it could easily be lost there. Sea control, or at least a sufficient degree of balance in these northern waters, can prove decisive for the ability of the Soviet Union to strike against NATO's transatlantic supply lines, as well as for protection of the Soviet northern base area in the Murmansk-Kola region, and for protection of the long-range ballistic missile submarines (DELTAs and TYPHOONs) which pose a direct strategic threat to North America from positions in the far north. The transatlantic supply lines, or the main artery for a NATO defense of Europe in a war of any duration, will be primary targets for Soviet attack just as they were for the German Navy in World War II and World War I.

In this context, control of the coasts, ports and airfields in the AFNORTH area may prove decisive for the ability to support allied maritime operations, or to harrass and prevent enemy maritime operations from the Barents Sea in the north to the Greenland-Iceland-United Kingdom gap and to the North Sea in the south. On the outbreak of a new Battle of the Atlantic, the powerful Soviet Northern Fleet, possibly supplemented by units from the Baltic Fleet, would play the major role against the alliance. Coastal control on the northern flank will be sought by both sides. For Norwegians at least, the submarine bunkers built by the Germans in Bergen and Trondheim are reminders of why their country had acquired a strategic importance which neutrality could neither prevent nor protect. Soviet admirals are no less concerned than were the German World War II admirals with securing optimum use and security for their vessels. For the alliance, it is equally important to maintain sufficient control on the northern flank for optimum advantage in an eventual maritime battle, for maximum deterrence of the Northern Fleet component of the Soviet nuclear strike capability and to live up to its fundamental obligation of protecting also its northern members against armed attack and to resist and repel attack if it were to occur. Toward these ends, maritime supply and support will be essential, though difficult.

Defense on the northern flank appears to be based on the general assumption that Soviet military strategy against NATO's northern flank will be aimed at securing the combined offensive and defensive capability of the Soviet Navy and expanding the defensive perimeter for bases and installations. In the far north, this could mean an attack by the 45th Motorized Infantry Division (stationed in the Petchenga-Murmansk area), supplemented by the 63rd Regiment of the (Northern Fleet) Marine Infantry. The attack could be reinforced by the 54th Motorized Infantry Division which is stationed between the Finnish border and the White Sea (between Alakurtti and Kandalaska) and other units in the 6th Army. Unless an attack on the Arctic Front were to be limited to a strictly localized conflict -- which Soviet planners might possibly hope for, but could not expect -- the northern strategic direction would have to be coordinated with a parallel or simultaneous drive against the Baltic approaches along the northern front in the European theater. The aim of that drive would be to open access for the Baltic Fleet. To secure its passage the strategy would call for an effort to gain control of airfields and ports in southeast Norway as well.

Allied defense in the AFNORTH area has been based on the assumption that northern Norway is most exposed to the Soviet threat. Thus the bulk of standing Norwegian forces are stationed in the north. An attack in the south will be met in the Danish region and would allow time for mobilization in south Norway. However, it should be pointed out that there is concern in some quarters about the ability to hold the Danish islands and to block passage of Soviet vessels. There is also some fear that a rapid Soviet strike against southeast Norway may be planned. Until recently it was assumed that western and middle Norway were protected by their distance from Soviet bases. But advancements in Soviet air capabilities, coupled with the valuable NATO targets there, suggest that this area could also be attacked -- complicating the defensive task.

An important question must be faced in Allied defense planning: will a Soviet attack in the far north be concentrated along the Soviet-Norwegian border, or will Soviet troops take the short-cut across northern Finland? It is a fact that Soviet roads and rail tracks do run in the east-to-west direction to the Finnish border and that several good Finnish roads lead to the Norwegian border. In this connection, it may also be mentioned that all Norwegian defense planners are not entirely happy concerning the new road which has recently been opened between Sweden and Norway (Kiruna-to-Narvik). This raises the question if and to what extent Soviet strategy against the NATO northern flank includes use of Finnish and Swedish territory, with the risk that those two countries will resist invasion and thus join the fight against Soviet forces. The possibility that not only Finland, but even Sweden may become involved cannot be excluded. Soviet activities in Swedish waters may indicate that planning in that direction is, in fact, taking place.

Finnish troops alone would hardly be able to deter for long a Soviet attack against Norway across northern Lapland. But assuming that Finnish troops would resist -- and no Soviet planner can exclude that possibility -- the move would add to the forces to be subdued, and it would create problems behind Soviet lines as the offensive advanced toward its real aim across the Norwegian, and NATO, border. Involvement of Sweden as well, would add very substantially to forces opposing the USSR. Soviet planning for that eventuality therefore must be based on the assumption that it will not be possible to keep neutral Sweden or neighbor Finland out of a war on the northern flank and consequently that it will be necessary in any event to subdue those countries as part of an offensive toward the west coast at the Scandinavian Peninsula.

The cost obviously would be very high, and Soviet strategists must act on the assumption that even a preparatory invasion in Finland and/or in Sweden before a direct attack upon NATO members would lead to immediate reactions on the NATO side, greatly reducing the chances of success in a continued campaign toward the west. While an attack upon either of the two could not by any stretch of the imagination be equalled to a direct, armed attack upon Denmark, enough reason exists for Denmark and for Norway to reconsider their self-imposed restrictions upon NATO defense and to open their territory for allied troops and possibly even for nuclear weapons.

"Nordic Balance"

There is an assumption -- particularly strong in Norway -- to the effect that the different status of the Nordic countries in security and defense policy creates, in effect, a stabilizing balance (the "Nordic Balance") between NATO and the Soviet Union in the northern region. In this view, Denmark's and Norway's membership in NATO, Sweden's policy of nonalignment in peace and of neutrality in war, and Finland's special agreement with the Soviet Union, singly and together, support that balance. The further assumption -- again particularly strong in Norway -- is that by maintaining restrictions upon NATO presence and activity, Norway and Denmark do not contribute to any armed threat against the Soviet Union. (It should be recalled that both Norway and Denmark, while members of NATO, do not permit foreign bases nor nuclear weapons in peacetime.) For that reason, the Soviet Union has no reason or justification for pressing Finland into military cooperation. Furthermore, because any Soviet measures against Finland -- or Sweden -- will upset the Nordic Balance and threaten Norway and Denmark, the Soviet Union will avoid steps which will be interpreted as a possible threat and lead to an escalation of defense preparations including an invitation of allied forces to be stationed in Scandinavia and preparation for the acceptance of nuclear arms.

Soviet Political Strategy in the North

With the awesome destructive power of nuclear weapons and the continuing certainty that attack upon one NATO member will be considered an attack upon all, the use of military force against the NATO northern flank, or against any state within the northern group, involves a risk of escalation which Soviet leaders quite obviously and sensibly are not prepared to take. Thus, while the military planners have prepared their strategies for the various thinkable and unthinkable contingencies, and keep developing their military means for pursuing those strategies if the need arises, political strategy appears to be the only practical, working tool for advancing Soviet strategic interests and goals in Northern Europe. In this respect the Clausewitzian principle that war is a continuation of politics by different means has been effectively reversed into a principle of gaining through diplomacy and political action that which cannot be had through the use of force. What then, is it that the Soviet Union wants in Northern Europe?

As far a Norway is concerned, a first indication of Soviet desires came when the Soviet government proved unwilling at first to accept the Spitsbergen Treaty of 1920, which recognized Norway's sovereignty in Svalbard. One primary cause of the Soviet opposition of course was that Russia had not participated in the negotiations at Versailles, when the victorious allies adopted the plan. Earlier negotiations on the status of Spitsbergen had pointed toward a tripartite regime (Norway, Sweden, and Russia), with no single sovereign, but U.S. opposition in particular had served to promote the idea that the islands should be controlled by one of the small non-warring countries in Northern Europe and notably by Norway. In any case, Spitsbergen could have a future strategic role which neither an agreement for non-use of the islands for war-like purposes nor control by a mere lilliput state like Norway would be able to check. Norwegian diplomacy, however, could have made use of an effective bait, and traded recognition of the Soviet government for Soviet accession to the Spitsbergen Treaty.

The Soviet Union has forced its strategic interest upon Finland, in a costly, but nevertheless effective move. Finland's independence was secured after World War I, but was threatened again as European history moved into its next major conflagration in 1939. Finland and the Soviet Union had signed a non-aggression treaty in 1932, but on October 5, 1939, Moscow requested new negotiations and on October 14 demanded that Finland cede to the Soviet Union Eastern Karelia, islands in the Gulf of Finland, and the Petsamo (now Pechenga) district on the Barents Sea coast. The move was clearly aimed at extending the defensive perimeter for Leningrad, just as were the demands put to Estonia and the subsequent occupation and inclusion of all three Baltic states (Estonia, Latvia, Lithuania) in the Soviet domain. When negotiations with Finland broke down, the Soviet attack followed at the end of November 1939. After inflicting heavy losses on the much stronger Red Army, Finland called on March 12, 1940, for armistice and gave up to the USSR the areas which had been demanded five months earlier, plus the Salla district midway between Karelia and Petsamo.

On November 12, 1944, Moscow demanded renegotiation of the Spitsbergen Treaty to establish a joint Soviet-Norwegian condominium in the islands, recognition of an equal right and obligation for both countries to defend the islands and to station troops there, and full cession of Bear Island midway between Svalbard and the Norwegian mainland to the Soviet Union. The demands were put in a dramatic, midnight meeting between Foreign Minister Molotov and Norwegian Foreign Minister Trygve Lie who was in Russia for a quite different matter, and they were justified by Molotov on the grounds that the Soviet Union absolutely had to have secure access to the Atlantic. He pointed out (banging his fist on a map), that the Soviet Union was blocked in the Dardanelles and the Danish straits and that the security of the Northern provinces could be decisive for the very existence of the Soviet Union.

Looking at the world from Moscow, the Scandinavian landmass forms a barrier to the North Atlantic. In one respect, it can serve as a protective shield against intrusion, at least if Moscow herself can maintain control of the maritime access routes into the Baltic and into the Barents Sea. However, if the Soviet Union cannot control the approaches, and that means control of the coasts for protection, the Scandinavian barrier will prevent the Soviet Union from having open and secure access to the world seas. In the period up to and through World War II, defensive interest was probably the main motive for the Soviet drive to secure the maritime approaches. The postwar period, however, has seen the Soviet Navy focus not only on maritime defense of the USSR but also on the offensive use of the Soviet Navy in distant waters. Since the Cuban Missile Crisis of 1962, Moscow has worked diligently to turn the USSR into a maritime superpower using all the elements of state seapower, i.e., the navy, the merchant marine, the fishing fleet, and the research vessels, to promote Soviet interests throughout the world.

In this new context, securing access to the sea has become a primary task for the Soviet Union. Thus, in addition to the war fighting capability of the Soviet Navy and the need to secure the homeland against attack from the sea as well as over land, a new and offensive maritime interest has emerged which will strongly influence Soviet policy toward its neighbors on the northern flank of the NATO area. Since the mid-1960s, Soviet naval exercises have followed a consistently more forward pattern pointing to the importance of the Norwegian Sea and the whole area north of the Greenland-Iceland-United Kingdom gap for strategic purposes.

As the Soviet Union continues to build up its capabilities for attacking the NATO northern flank, and as it becomes more self-assured about these capabilities, it may be inclined toward more impetuous political behavior toward the area. One can hope, though, that the Soviet feeling of military strength will be tempered by an adequate understanding of interdependence and of the need for cooperation with states other than those which Moscow regards as "friendly" if the full potential for economic development in the north is to be realized. In this respect, the NATO northern flank area will, as noted earlier, offer a rather unique opportunity for the East and the West alike to learn to develop new potentials alongside each other, with practical cooperation when possible and mutually advantageous, and with full mutual respect for the integrity of each other's territories and sovereign rights in designated zones. A minimum requirement for that to happen is that there be no use of force nor the threat to use force, nor efforts to interfere with the policies of the states on the northern flank.

Chapter 11

SOVIET POLITICAL STRATEGY
TOWARD THE FEDERAL REPUBLIC OF GERMANY

Wolfgang Seiffert

Introduction

The division of Germany will be viewed here as a given fact, and its origins and consequences will only be discussed insofar as they may contribute to an understanding of Soviet strategy towards the Federal Republic of Germany (FRG). The topic to be dealt with here is of a considerably more limited nature. We are concerned with Soviet strategy toward the FRG, or West Germany, and this predominantly in terms of the present. In this approach, we are not concerned with military strategy, but rather with political strategy.

The concept of strategy is taken from the art of war, which can be understood as the planning for and leadership of large units. It reflects the character of communist parties in that they act like paramilitary, conspiratorial organizations[1] and in that they conduct all of their activities, including those involving international relations, using terms and concepts borrowed from the military. They generally understand this practice as part of the "strategy and tactics of the revolutionary worker's movement," whereby political strategy is understood as "determining the direction of the main thrust" as well as the "relationship to the different social forces in a given period of societal development."[2] Projected onto foreign policy concerns, political strategy means: "to define the principles, tasks, and goals . . . in the sphere of international relations . . . as well as the means and methods of their realization."[3]

At the center of Soviet foreign policy/strategy lies the general concept of "consistent change in the international power relationship."[4] From the Soviet point of view, the struggle for power by individual nation states and the concept of a balance of power has, since 1917, been replaced by the global conflict between two different social systems. To change the balance of power in favor of world socialism, which is the central focus of Soviet foreign policy, follows as a natural consequence of these deliberations.[5]

When we speak, therefore, of a political strategy of the Soviet Union towards the FRG, we mean that the USSR maintains a political concept (objective) vis-a-vis the FRG, a concept which encompasses the main thrust of its policies, as well as the methods and means by which these are to be realized: in other words, a combined plan of action and policy.

This preliminary thesis does not mean that a plan has to be worked out to develop measures dealing with every aspect that may arise, or that this concept is itself unchangeable and is not subject to modification or accommodation. What it means is that the Soviet Union has fixed goals for its policies towards the FRG, goals it steadfastly pursues. Soviet strategy takes into consideration the real and changing conditions for the realization of its policies in the international arena, in the FRG, as well as in the world of socialist states and inside the Soviet Union. In this connection, it is prudent to caution against the view that the Soviet Union would, because of government-level relations with the FRG, abandon its control of the DKP (German Communist Party in the FRG) or its policy of influencing other political parties, groups, or persons which appear suitable to its ends in the FRG. The exact opposite is the case.

The FRG's Existence: A Defeat for Moscow

The Soviet Union proceeds from the understanding that the Germany which it defeated together with the Western allies is today divided but that the German question itself has not really been solved. Austria reemerged as an independent state, and a union with Germany was forbidden in Article 2 of the 1955 "Staatsvertrag" quadripartite treaty. The eastern territories of Germany which went to the Soviet Union and Poland have, on the one hand, become more secure for the USSR as seizin, legally possessed land. This benefit is a result of the declaration in the various treaties with Warsaw Pact states concerning the "inviolability of borders" and of the Final Act of the Helsinki Conference (1975). On the other hand, these territories would fall in terms of international law under the proviso of a peace treaty with a reunified Germany. Although the German Democratic Republic (GDR), or East Germany, has been integrated into the Warsaw Pact and COMECON and displays greater stability in comparison to other East European states, the attraction of the FRG's economic power and the appeal of its political and cultural life to the Germans in the GDR have remained consistent. The currently high number of applications for exit visas by GDR citizens attests to this fact.

According to Soviet analyses, the FRG has developed into an economic power which can count itself among the three leading industrial nations of the world; it represents the dominant power in the European Community, the strongest force in NATO after the United States and, with the stationing of Pershing II and cruise missiles, has become a starting ramp for American missiles aimed at the Soviet Union.[6] The 1971 quadripartite settlement concerning Berlin also created, from the Soviet point of view, a "cleansing of the atmosphere" and represented a "rational balance of the interests of all interested parties."[7] Nevertheless, the free section of Berlin in the middle of the GDR remains a problem for the Soviet Union.

The Soviet Union will take any measures needed to maintain the Group of Soviet Armed Forces in Germany stationed in the GDR and Berlin, along with their reinforcement troops in Poland. Countermeasures of various sorts to be taken against the FRG in case of conflict will be mounted from the territory of the GDR and Czechoslovakia. It is clear that the Warsaw Pact agreements will be extended indefinitely.[8]

After the Potsdam Conference in 1945 and after taking a variety of differing initial positions, the Soviet Union adopted the line that Germany had to be impeded from ever again being able to threaten the Soviet Union militarily[9] and that there were two alternative ways of attaining this goal: a Germany that was autonomous but more or less dependent on the Soviet Union, or a separate communist state carved out by the division of Germany. Initially both alternatives were pursued simultaneously, whereby Stalin and his successors, Malenkov and Beria, preferred Germany's national unity; in the early 1950s this became coupled with the concept of armed neutrality. Subsequently, both variations have been adhered to by the Soviet Union. Since the formation of the FRG, however, the idea of Germany's national unity (regardless of its form) has only been actively suggested by Moscow when the USSR wanted to respond to what Moscow perceived to be negative developments in the FRG (1952-1955, 1959). At the same time such suggestions were regularly coupled with internal problems in the East Bloc or in the USSR, and with power struggles within the Soviet leadership. The one or the other variant was, however, invariably an expression of the same power-political conception of the Soviet Union aimed at getting Germany under its control.[10]

With the founding of the FRG, a Western political strategy emerged which strove to integrate the new state irreversibly into the West's political, military, and economic alliance and system of values.[11] The results and improvements arising from this integration have been to the West's advantage, and they are well known. Despite the economic and military potential of the GDR, understood by the Soviet Union as the FRG's counterpart, it does not provide a sufficient or lasting equivalent to the FRG. Under these conditions, the existence of the FRG must continue to appear to the Soviet Union as a painful defeat of its strategy towards Germany.

Recognizing Realities and Maintaining Old Options

Since the FRG's integration into the North Atlantic Treaty Organization (NATO), the USSR has ceased to include questions concerning the national unity of Germany as part of the Soviet operative policy towards Germany, but rather has entrusted this to its deputy, the GDR, which until 1968 officially held to the goal of a unified communist Germany.[12] Although the Soviet Union itself recognized the realities, it held to its previous desires: no military threat from German territory, the inviolability of borders, and having the whole of Germany under its influence.

In the foreground emerged an offensive status-quo policy which was based on the two-state theory and which pursued a cementing of the German division without being satisfied with the status quo as such. The policy aimed at a removal of Berlin's special status, and if it ever considered a reunification of Germany, it was only for one under communist rule.[13] Within the framework of this concept, Moscow held to its goal of a German peace settlement until 1964.[14]

That the Soviet Union took the initiative in 1955 in establishing diplomatic relations with the FRG is compatible with this concept of an offensive status-quo policy. In this way, the Soviet Union wanted to underscore demonstratively its _seizin_ in Germany and, by establishing direct ties, wanted at the same time to develop new possibilities and ways of influencing the FRG. As a result of the diplomatic recognition negotiations with the FRG, the Soviet Union nevertheless had to accept the provisos of non-recognition of all territorial changes in East Europe and of the FRG's right to all-German representation, as well as expressly recognize that the major national problem of the German people remains the re-establishment of Germany's national unity.[15]

The assumption of diplomatic relations between both states could neither fulfill the FRG's hope for improved relations with the Soviet Union, nor enable the Soviet Union to attain the goals it sought in establishing relations.[16] Consequently, the Soviet Union concentrated on the continued integration of the GDR into the Eastern alliance, as well as on the GDR's security, which resulted in 1961 in the building of the Berlin Wall.[17] Relations between Bonn and Moscow deteriorated, and Soviet policy towards Germany, in questions about Germany and Europe as a whole, became inflexible.

Nevertheless, the assumption of diplomatic relations brought with it a number of positive consequences for both sides: a normalization of relations was initiated. A long-term agreement on goods and payment transactions, an agreement on general questions of shipping and trade, and a consular agreement were signed. In 1959, both sides reached an agreement concerning cultural, technological, and economic exchange. Overall, the Soviet Union has, however, been frustrated, in terms of long-range success, in its attempts to achieve its fundamental goals.

Bonn's Ostpolitik Seen by Moscow as an Opportunity

The USSR's policy towards Germany as a whole, the leadership change in the FRG government from Ludwig Erhard to the "grand coalition" (1966), and then even more the forming of the Brandt/Scheel government (1969) along with its announcement of a new Ostpolitik,[18] must have appeared to the Soviet Union as its great chance to take decisive steps towards the realization of its political strategy towards the FRG. In fact, Soviet authors appraised this development as the "collapse of the CDU/CSU's (Christian Democratic Union/Christian Socialist Union) foreign policy course,"[19] and judged the Moscow Treaty, signed by the new Brandt/Scheel government on August 12, 1970,[20] as an "event of first-rate political significance"[21] which would introduce a "shift towards realism in the policies of the FRG."[22]

Indeed the Soviet Union did achieve through the Moscow Treaty an improved safeguard of its seizin, a stabilization of the status quo, and an improved basis from which to extend its influence over the FRG and over West Europe itself. New agreements were subsequently reached: an agreement concerning the development and consolidation of long-term cooperation in the fields of economy and industry, an air traffic agreement, and finally a cultural agreement. During talks between Chancellor Brandt and Soviet Party Secretary Brezhnev in the Crimea in 1971, an understanding was reached that the activities of the DKP, founded in 1968 in the FRG, would not be penalized with prohibitive measures.[23]

It cannot be overlooked that the 1970 Moscow Treaty has nevertheless had a modus-vivendi character and has afforded the FRG more freedom of action in world politics, a freedom the FRG has used to advantage. The inviolability of existing borders, which the Moscow Treaty obligates its signatory parties to, does not exclude any mutual and peaceful change in the status quo. And it does not constitute a border treaty, but rather a renunciation of force treaty. The same is true of the FRG's adherence to its goal of German unity. Moreover, an exchange of notes made expressly clear that the rights and responsibilities of the Four Powers concerning Berlin and Germany as a whole would not be affected.[24]

The Soviet Union's attempt to make a decisive step towards an improved safeguarding of its seizin within the framework of the new Ostpolitik was, therefore, only to a limited extent successful. Moreover, the USSR's efforts to achieve a military superiority in Europe,[25] by means of an extensive SS-20 missile program parallel to its so-called policy of detente, proved to be counterproductive.

The controversy surrounding the NATO rearmament program ended in Soviet defeat: The FRG Parliament voted by a majority for the basing of U.S. intermediate-range missiles, and the coalition government of the CDU/CSU and the Free Democrats began stationing the new missiles without delay.

With the conclusion in 1972 of the Treaty Concerning the Basis for Relations Between the FRG and the GDR,[26] the GDR, on the one hand, achieved (for the most part) the international recognition it sought; on the other hand, inner-German relations retained their special character and were officially set on the basis of a mutual respect for the existence of two states in Germany.[27] The solidarity among Germans as a nation was strengthened, and the intensified relations between the two German states supported ambitions, existing within the GDR leadership, for more autonomy.[28]

Soviet Propaganda, the Peace Movement, and the FRG

Since the end of 1983, the Soviet Union has been conducting a propaganda campaign against the FRG in order to exert political pressure. By internationally describing the FRG as revanchist and aggressive, the Soviet Union hopes to initiate a return to the status quo existing prior to the 1979 NATO decision to place the U.S. intermediate-range PERSHING II and cruise missiles in Europe, or at least to achieve some modifications in the missile program.

This Soviet position vis-a-vis the FRG is only understandable when seen as part of Moscow's global strategy towards the West. The USSR believes that the United States has begun an all-out effort to delimit Soviet power in all areas of the globe and to reduce its status to one of a European and Asian power only.[29] Accordingly, Moscow deems it essential that the overall strategic nuclear parity of the USSR with the United States (as recognized by President Nixon in 1972) be maintained, under all circumstances and with all means available, and remain irreversible.[30] This task is to be subordinate to all other objectives concerning states in the Warsaw Pact and COMECON. He who believes that the Soviet Union is only or most concerned about closing open questions and holes in the European order in accordance with Soviet interests, about breaking the awakening national consciousness among Germans, or about preventing the possible consequences of a rapprochement between the two German states that may have gone too far, has certainly misread Moscow's scale of priorities. Its top priority is to prevent the demise of the USSR as a superpower.[31]

Seen from this perspective, the deployment of Pershing II and cruise missiles in West Europe is, above and beyond its military effect, an important part of the American policy of delimiting Soviet power. With its assent to the missiles, the FRG is, on the one hand, the most important European country for the realization of American policy. On the other hand, the Soviet leadership was convinced that by preventing the missiles from being stationed in the FRG, their stationing could be prevented throughout the rest of Europe. Soviet policy cannot, therefore, be denied a certain amount of logic when it sees a prevention of the missiles from being stationed in the FRG (or their later dismantling) as the key to foiling American policy in the whole of Europe.

The Soviet leadership obviously proceeds from the assumption that this goal cannot be attained with the help of the peace movement in the FRG alone, but it regards the struggle for this goal as neither concluded, nor possible to be abandoned.[32] The Soviet leadership depends on the fact that the deployment has itself just begun in West Europe and will take a long time. Moscow hopes that during this period the popular movements motivated by fear and concern against deployment in all West European countries will break out again. It banks on a radicalization of the relations between government and opposition and on increasing differences between the different member states within NATO -- a process which can be furthered by Soviet pressure on NATO countries.

Above all, the Soviet Union is determined to put more and more political and propagandistic pressure on the FRG. Its argumentation is ultimately geared toward drawing a distorted picture of the FRG for the international public, a picture showing the Federal Republic preparing for war which would entail violation of the Moscow Treaty of 1970 and justify an application of the enemy state clauses of Articles 53 and 107 of the United Nations Charter.[33] Moscow argues that the United States, together with the other NATO countries, supports and indeed promotes the revival of aggressive intentions, revanchism, militarism, and fascism in the FRG.[34] Through such arguments, a specious legitimation for one-sided Soviet measures against the Federal Republic, justified on the basis of the enemy state clauses, has been created. Whether or not Moscow acts to support its declared positions will, of course, depend ultimately on how the Soviet leadership weighs the risks of acting. It is to be expected that the Soviet Union will intensify its policy toward the FRG up to the point of threatening military force, including demonstrative maneuvers, reinforcements, and counter-deployment in the GDR and Czechoslovakia, as well as threats against the FRG supposedly justified by the enemy state clauses.

Shifting Role of the FRG in Soviet Strategy

Under these circumstances, the status of the FRG in Soviet global strategy has changed. In the years from 1969-1980, the FRG was practically the most privileged partner in Western Europe, but now Soviet relations with the FRG are being consciously downgraded, in order to demonstrate that Moscow can also exist without the FRG. This tendency is especially emphasized by the fact that in May 1985 the Soviet Union celebrated the fortieth anniversary of the victory over Hitler's Germany as a major political event. Moscow sought to show the FRG that its relations with the other states of the Warsaw Pact, including the GDR, can only be as good as its relations with Moscow. Whatever its words and actions, Moscow recognizes that in the future the FRG will remain the most important country for the Soviet Union in West Europe, the focus upon which the Soviet Union has to concentrate its efforts if it wants to make progress in its policy towards Europe.

The prospects of reestablishing the dialogue with the United States could nourish Soviet hopes that an agreement could be reached with the United States without giving deference to the Europeans. U.S.-Soviet arms control agreements are today only conceived in long and difficult negotiations and are limited to a few certain areas. Agreements which do not sufficiently allow for the European interests, because they accept a certain Soviet military superiority, are no longer possible. This compels the Soviet Union to reconsider its strategy towards the FRG. Which line this strategy will take is a question to be considered in the perspective of German-Soviet relations in their entirety.

Results and Perspectives of Soviet Policy Towards Germany

The balance of the Soviet policy towards Germany is, despite all defeats, by no means without results. With the founding of the GDR, a Soviet-styled communist system was established within the German nation, although the state was limited to the territory of the Soviet zone of occupation. With the Moscow Treaty of 1970, the Soviet Union obtained a political and legal basis for direct relations with the political leaders in the other German state and for opportunities to influence the FRG's development. With the Basic Treaty of 1972 between the GDR and the FRG, the actual recognition of the GDR as a state within Germany was achieved, and thus the lever of communist influence on developments in Germany was strengthened. Admittedly, at present the Soviet Union and the GDR confine themselves to aligning their relations to the FRG according to the principle of peaceful coexistence. But this principle is understood as a long-term truce in which the spreading of communism should follow, if possible, without war.

The successive steps of the long-range strategy of the Soviet Union towards Germany remain, thereby, unchanged: the establishment of the GDR state; the loosening of the FRG's relations to the United States and the Western Alliance; the complete equality of the GDR with the FRG; and then finally, manifesting the claim that the communists and their German state are the actual heirs and proponents of German history.

In this balance, two debit items in the Soviet Union's relations to Bonn show especially unfavorably in the USSR's books. One item is the integration of the FRG into the Western military alliance, the other is the as yet unfinalized provision of the territorial status quo. In the years ahead, the security interests of the Soviet Union (which, according to their self-concept, go far beyond the legitimate interests of any state in order to ensure its own defense), will necessitate increased efforts both to loosen the FRG's relations with NATO, and to reduce the FRG's importance within the Western military alliance. Those aims will be at the center of Soviet strategy towards Germany. Closely connected with this is the demand for the inviolability of the territorial status quo.[35] This Gromyko already emphasized at the signing of the Moscow Treaty:

> The border question has been decided by war and post-war developments. The borders are recognized, they are taken into account, and not only European countries operate on the basis of their existence. The unassailability of the Western borders of the socialist union of states will be guaranteed by the entire power of the USSR and its allies.[36]

Thus both the question of Soviet security interests and of the unassailability of the territorial status quo will continue to govern the political strategy of the Soviet Union towards the FRG.

The chances are limited for the Soviet Union to advance in these questions with the existing strategy of political pressure, political downgrading of relations, and threats. Moreover, the advantages of the division of Germany, which have been enjoyed by the Soviet Union to their full extent, are gradually becoming exhausted and are actually turning into disadvantages.

This situation will hardly cause the Soviet Union to switch quickly to a strategy geared towards a restoration of Germany's national unity. Such a new strategy would raise grave problems for the Soviet Union and for its role as a hegemonic power in the group of East European states.[37] Given the drastically changed situation in Europe and Germany, it could scarcely be a matter of a simple return to the policy of an autonomous but neutral Germany dependent on the Soviet Union. Indeed, the dream of a reunified Germany as political superpower in the present world is forever destroyed, but if the Soviet Union wishes to count on the success of a new strategy it will have to show its willingness to accept a free Germany as a self-determining Central European power, which is free in its internal affairs, integrated into the European Community, and militarily aligned with the Western alliance.

142

NOTES

1. Vgl. z. B. dazu: Wolfgang Seiffert
Die Sozialistiche Einheitspartei Deutschlands (SED) -
Zentrum der Herrschaftsordnung in der DDR
Manuskript, Kiel 1984
2. Vgl. Kleines politisches Worterbuch, 3. Auflage,
Berlin (Ost) 1978, S. 888
3. Worterbuch der Außenpolitik und des Volkerrechts
Berlin (Ost) 1980, S. 64
4. G.H. Sachnazarov
K probleme sootnosenija sil v mire, in: Kommunist (Moskau)
1974, H. 3, S. 77-89
5. Eduard Pestel
Prinzipien und Triebkrafte sowjetischer Außenpolitik
in: Das sowjetische Konzept der Korrelation der Krafte
und seine Anwendung auf die Aubenpolitik, Hamburg,
S. 295-306
6. Vgl. Lew Besymenski
Im Schatten amerikanischer Raketen
Prawda (Moskau) v. 27. Juli 1984, deutsch in:
Deutschland-Archiv, H. 9/1984, S. 993-997
7. P.A. Abrassimow
Wesberlin gestern und heute
Berlin (Ost) 1981, S. 168 ff.;
V.N. Belezki, a.a.O. (FN 3), S. 351
8. Vgl. Wolfgang Seiffert
Die Moskauer "Revanchismus"-Vorwurfe und die Gultigkeits-
klauseln des Warschauer Paktes, in: Deutschland-Archiv 9/1984,
S. 900-903 sowie das Interview DER SPIEGEL vom 3. Dezember
1984 mit Sagladin
9. V.N. Belezki
Die Politik der Sowjetunion in den deutschen Angelegenheiten
in der Nachkriegszeit 1945-1976, Berlin (Ost) 1977
10. Boris Meissner (Hrsg. und Einleitung), Moskau-Bonn
Die Beziehungen zwischen der Sowjetunion und der
Bundesrepublik Deutschland 1955-1973, Koln 1975, Bd. I, S.11; Vgl.
Georg von Rauch/Boris Meissner Die deutsch-sowjetischen
Beziehungen - Von 1917 bis 1967 - Wurzburg 1967, S. 21-19.
11. B. Meissner
Moskau - Bonn, a.a.O. (FN 10), Bd. I, S. 11
12. W. Seiffert
SED und nationale Frage, in: W. Venohr (Hrsg.),
Die deutsche Einheit kommt bestimmt
Bergisch-Gladbach 1982, S. 161-179
13. B. Meissner
Die deutsch-sowjetischen Beziehungen von 1941 bis 1967,

a.a.O. (FN 10), S. 21

14. Vgl. z. B. die Rede des sowjetischen Partiesekretars
L.I. Breschnew vom 6. November 1964; auszugsweise Wiedergabe
in B. Meissner, Moskau - Bonn, a.a.O. (FN 10), Bd. II,
S. 1016

15. B. Meissner
Die deutsch-sowjetischen Beziehungen, a.a.O. (FN 10), S. 32
Moskau - Bonn, Bd. I a.a.O. (FN 10), S. 19/20;
Gemeinsames deutsch-sowjetisches SchuBkomminique
uber die Vanhandlungen zwischen der Sowjetunion und der
Bundesrepublik Deutschland vom 13. September 1955

16. V.N. Belezki
Die Politik der Sowjetunion ..., a.a.O. (FN 9), S. 185

17. B. Meissner
Moskau - Bonn, a.a.O. (FN 10) Bd. I, S. 48

18. Vgl. die Darstellung bei B. Meissner,
Moskau - Bonn, a.a.O. (FN 10), Bd. II, S. 775-795

19. V.N. Belezki
Die Politik der Sowjetunion, a.a.O. (FN 9), S. 324

20. Text in: B. Meissner, Moskau - Bonn a.a.O. (FN 10), S.
1270-1271

21. V.N. Belezki
Die Politik der Sowjetunion, a.a.O. (FN 9), S. 340

22. Zitiert bei B. Meissner
Moskau - Bonn, a.a.O. (FN 10), Bd. II, S. 1559/61,
1622-2423.

23. Es versteht sich, daB in dem offiziellen Komminuque
hiervon keine Rede ist

24. B. Meissner
Moskau - Bonn, a.a.O. (FN 10), Bd. II, S. 789

25. Wolfgang Seiffert
Die sowjetische Konzeption der militar-stratigschen
Paritat, in: Zeitschrift fur Politik, H. 4/1984

26. Bundesgestzblatt 1973, Teil II, S. 421 ff.

27. Vgl. Wolfgang Seiffert
Die Begriffe "Anerkennung" und "Respektierung" in den
innerdeutschen Beziehungen, in: Recht in Ost und West,
Heft 2/1984, S. 49-60

28. derselbe, Die Natur des Konflikts zwischen SED und
Moskau,
in: Deutschland Archiv H. 10/1984, S. 1043-1059

29. Vgl. z. B. Die Rede des USA-AuBenministers G. Schultz
vor dem 15. Congressional Testimony vom 15. Juni 1982; die Rede
des US -Vizeprasidenten George Bush vor der Gesellschaft fur
AuBenpolitik und internationale Beziehungen in der Wiener Hofburg
am 21. September 1983, herausgegeben vom US-Information Service
der US-Botschaft in Wien; die Rede von Ronald Reagan am Vorabend

der KVAE-Konferenz in Stockholm, deutscher Text in: Frankfurter
Rundschau vom 19. Januar 1984, S. 15; die Rede von Shultz zur
Eroffnung der KVAE-Konferenz.
  30. Dies war z. B. das Resumee des Gesprachs zwischen
McGovern
und Gromyko im Juli 1984; vgl. Die Welt von Juli 1984, S. 2
  31. Fritjof Meyer
Weltmacht im Absteig - Der Niedergang der Sowjet-Union,
Munchen, 1984
  32. Vgl. den wohl vor allem an die westdeutsche
Friedensbewegung
gerichteten Artikel des Mitarbeiters der ZK-Abteilung der
KPdSU, N. Portugalow, in den Blatter(n) fur internationale Politik,
Koln, Heft 6/1984, S. 683 ff.: "Atlantische Gotter-
dammerung - Die USA, Westeuropa und die Rolle der NATO."
  33. Eine neue, ausfuhrliche politikwissenschaftliche
Untersuchung
der Problematik der Feinstaatenklauseln, findet such bei
Monica H. Forbes, Feindstaatenklauseln, Viermachteverant-
wortung und Deutsche Frage, Ebenhausen 1983
  34. Mitteilung uber das Treffen zwischen Tschernenko und
Honecker, in: Neues Deutschland vom 15. Juni 1984, S. 1
  35. Vgl. auch A. A. Gromyko
Uber die internationale Lage und die AuBenpolitik der Sowjetunion,
in Neues Deutschland vom 18./19. Juni 1983, S. 5/6.
  36. zitiert bei B. Meissner, Moskau - Bonn, a. a. O. (FN 10)
Bd. II, S. 803.
  37. Zur Entwichlung in dieser Straatengruppe vgl. J. Hacker,
Der Ostblock, Baden-Baden 1983

Chapter 12

RESOURCE WAR IN SOVIET GLOBAL STRATEGY

James Arnold Miller

The indirect but ever-present threat increasingly being posed to industrialized nations by Moscow's projection of military and economic power is its resource war. The Soviet goal is to separate the industrialized states from their foreign sources of vital or strategic materials, and disrupt sealanes through which these resources move, thus weakening the industrialized states and hastening the ultimate victory of Moscow-brand socialism over capitalism.

Within the framework of their overall global strategy, the Soviet planners are opportunistic, yet cautious, as they seek to exploit any instabilities or weaknesses in nations, especially the developing nations in the so-called Third World, that are suppliers of the resources. These developing nations may be seen as a global point of vulnerability, a kind of "soft underbelly," through which Moscow can indirectly weaken the economics of West Europe, the United States, and Japan.

Natural Resources Denial/Disruption

A major element of Soviet global strategy, inadequately recognized by many Americans, West Europeans, and Japanese, is a persistent effort to increase the USSR's ability to manipulate or control the flow to the industrialized nations of strategic resources, both nonfuel and energy.[1]

Robert Moss, former editor of the "Foreign Report" intelligence bulletin of the Economist magazine of London, commented on the importance of strategic resources in terms of attaining Soviet politico-military objectives:

Leonid Brezhnev told a secret meeting of Warsaw Pact leaders in Prague in 1973 that the Soviet objective was world dominance by the year 1985, and that the control of Europe's sources of energy and raw materials would reduce it to the condition of a hostage to Moscow.[2]

The Soviet leaders were overly optimistic about the time frame, but it is abundantly clear that resources competition is an integral element of Moscow's strategy against NATO. From Moscow's viewpoint, a resource war is low-cost, low-casualty, low-visibility, and usually below the threshold of effective West European or NATO response. It is noteworthy that NATO's mandate does not include any commitment to defend those strategic places from which critical energy and nonfuel mineral resources are extracted, nor those strategic places through or near which the resources are transported to the industrialized democracies. As Frank R. Barnett has pointed out, the undeclared resource war being waged by Moscow does not put at risk the population, farms, and factories of Mother Russia, and may not even interrupt the West-to-East flow of grain, technology, and credits. Aided by its modern four-ocean navy capable of wreaking havoc among the West's vital sealanes, and supported by Cuban, East German, and other proxy forces, the Soviet Union has in effect virtually encircled the petroleum of the Middle East and the nonfuel minerals of Southern Africa.[3]

As the means of production of nonfuel minerals, energy resources, and other products in resource-rich countries are increasingly coming under the ownership of governments, particularly socialism-oriented governments, the Soviet Union is being provided with an important opportunity to increase its influence at the expense of the West. This situation involves the decreased role played by free market forces and the decreased decision-making role of Western firms and governments, and it involves the enhanced ability of the Soviet Union to create special trading relationships through the Council for Mutual Economic Assistance (CMEA or COMECON) with state-owned raw materials monopolies.[4]

Clearly a major strategic aim of the Soviet Union in the developing nations is the creation or support of central economies and the decline or elimination of free enterprise. Tactical considerations often cause Moscow to encourage radical regimes to develop or maintain links to Western markets, foreign assistance, and international financial institutions. In so doing, the radical regimes will likely mute their revolutionary rhetoric. An example of "flexibility" on the part of a Soviet client state is the Marxist state of Angola, which has strong military ties with Moscow and a large Cuban troop presence. Indeed, Angola, Zimbabwe, and Mozambique are following the example of the Soviet Union in seeking Western investment and trade relationships while remaining dedicated to the ultimate eradication of capitalism wherever it exists. Not only West Europe, but also the United States, Japan, China/Taiwan (ROC), and South Korea are targets.

Closing in on Oil Supplies

U.S. government officials in recent years have expressed concerns about the Soviet Union's desires to deny or disrupt the flow of oil from the Persian Gulf area to the United States, West Europe, and Japan, as well as perhaps to seize the oil for its own use. For example, Secretary of Defense Harold Brown stated in May 1977 that, "the USSR might attempt to deny access to the oil of the Persian Gulf by direct attack on the facilities of the major oil loading ports which lie near to Soviet territory." He further noted that, "Simultaneous action to interdict on the high seas tanker movement of oil from other exporting nations could vastly exacerbate the oil supply situation of the United States and its allies."[5]

There has been underway an almost constant debate among specialists on energy and the Middle East about oil production and reserves, and the role of the Soviet Union. Many reports agree that in the late-1980s the Soviet Union, despite being the world's largest producer of oil, might be forced to become a net importer of oil. Thus Moscow, already short of hard currency, would be more inclined to use politico-military means to obtain access to oil supplies. Reasons given for the coming oil net-importer status for the Soviet Union include a slowing in the growth rate of all types of energy, increased domestic and CMEA demand, high rates of oil depletion, insufficient technology, and inadequate capital investment.[6]

Some experts believe that the Strait of Hormuz would be very difficult for Iran or any other nation or entity to close completely by military action. They say that the strait is too wide and too deep, with too many shipping lanes to be effectively blocked. The 17-mile-long strait averages about 50 miles in width and is about 30 miles wide at its narrowest point. Specialists disagree on how effective mining of the strait could be. Besides interdiction of the strait, another possibility is, of course, attacks on oil and other shipping inside the Persian Gulf itself.[7] The numerous attacks by Iraqi and Iranian aircraft on tankers and other ships in the gulf in recent years as an offshoot of their war has caused considerable anxiety in the oil-importing nations, and may portend worse developments there or elsewhere.[8] Also very significant was the 1984 mining of the Red Sea, reportedly by agents of Libya, presenting us with what one observer called "terrorism's new weapon."[9]

In West Europe, Italy relies on Persian Gulf oil for 45 percent of its needs, France 30 percent, and West Germany 15 percent. Japan, on the other hand, must obtain 52 percent of its requirements from Persian Gulf states.[10]   The most immediate effect of a disruption, according to a Congressional Research Service study of September 1983, would be a "sharp increase in the price of all oil supplies.[11]   The attackers could create at minimum psychological and symbolic effects, if not physical or material damage."[12]   The prospects for such disruption (actual or threatened attacks against oil shipping, by military commandos or terrorists) are heightened by the increased Soviet presence in the Persian Gulf region, and by Moscow's commitment to fomenting much more violence inimical to Western interests.

The Soviet invasion of Afghanistan in December 1979, and the continued presence there of over 115,000 Soviet troops, not only indicates Moscow's willingness to use brutal military force to achieve objectives, but also to put Soviet forces within 300 miles of the Persian Gulf. On the Arabian Peninsula, South Yemen, Moscow's ally, directs subversion and covert operations at Saudi Arabia, at Oman, and at other Persian Gulf oil-producing states.   The thousand-plus Cuban and East German military and security advisers in South Yemen, backed by Soviet forces, reportedly helped train and arm the Saudi and foreign rebels who occupied Mecca's Grand Mosque in Saudi Arabia in November 1979.[13]

Nonfuel Minerals and the Soviet Threat

Nonfuel minerals, like energy resources, are vital to modern industrial economies. For example, cobalt alloys are used heavily in jet engines, gas turbines, and permanent magnets. Substitution for cobalt is possible in some applications, but it is time-consuming, expensive, and in many cases results in significant loss of weight or other advantages. Manganese, an essential hardener and purifier of steel, has no satisfactory substitute in its major applications. Chromium is indispensable in making stainless steel which is used in hardened and specialty steels. Yet there is no known substitute for chromium in stainless steel. Nor is there a good alternative for chromium in industrial hard plating. Platinum is used in catalytic converters for automobiles, and it is also indispensable in the petroleum and chemical industries. Substitution of platinum and other platinum group metals is technically feasible but requires heavy capitalization, very long lead-time and full government support.[14]

In the event of significant disruptions in the supply of these four minerals to industrial users, substitution generally can provide only long-term and imperfect relief. Little relief can be provided through recycling: negligible relief for manganese, about 10 percent each for cobalt and chromium, and about 19 percent for platinum group metals, when considering percentage of U.S. consumption. And because of the tremendous costs, yet imperfect technology, decade-plus lead-time, and the lack of a satisfactory international legal regime, deep seabed mining to obtain such minerals as cobalt, manganese, copper, and nickel will not provide relief any time soon to the nonfuel minerals import-dependency problems of West Europe and the other industrialized democracies.[15]

By an accident of geology and geography, the Soviet Union and Southern Africa together control virtually all of the reserves of several nonfuel minerals that are indispensable to the economies of West Europe, as well as of the United States and Japan. This fact rightly leads to concern about the consequences if the Soviet Union ever gained direct, or even indirect, control over the mineral reserves and production of Southern Africa. The Soviet Union and Southern Africa account for the following percentages of world reserves: platinum group metals (99), manganese (98), vanadium (97), chromium (96), diamonds (87), gold (69), and cobalt (25). And in terms of current world production of these minerals, the Soviet Union and Southern Africa combined account for these percentages: platinum group metals (95), manganese (59), vanadium (60), chromium (57), diamonds (65), gold (80), and cobalt (74).[16]

There can be no doubt that the Soviet Union has the long-term specific aim of gaining effective control over the nonfuel mineral resources of Southern Africa, especially of South Africa. There is in effect already somewhat of a cartel in cobalt involving Zambia and Zaire, which accounted for some 60 percent of world production in each of 1983 and 1984.[17] Zambia presently has a radical government on friendly terms with the Soviet Union. In 1979, Zambia and the USSR signed a barter agreement worth $89 million to provide Soviet MiG jets and other weapons in return for Zambian cobalt. Zaire is presently generally pro-Western in orientation but the severely depressed economy, endemic poverty, and widespread popular dissension could prompt a major political upheaval which the USSR would certainly try to exploit.

If the Soviet Union controlled directly or even indirectly the minerals production and reserves of Southern Africa, it would be in a position to obtain political and economic concessions from the industrialized West. Moscow could manipulate supplies of a single commodity to a single Western industrialized country, or supplies of several commodities to several Western countries. What is being suggested here is a supercartel being created and manipulated by the Kremlin leaders on behalf of the economic, military, and political-ideological objectives of Soviet global strategy.

The key element in any Soviet-controlled multimineral supercartel in Southern Africa would be the coming to power in

South Africa of a radical government. It should be stressed that there are those who say that even a Marxist-run South Africa, in order to obtain vitally needed hard currency earnings, would have to sell to the West the nation's manganese, chromium, and platinum group metals. But these commodities, despite their critical and strategic importance to Western end-users, amount, on average, to less than 10 percent of the annual export sales of South Africa's minerals industry. Indeed, based on recent statistics from the South African Minerals Bureau, exports of chrome ore and ferrochrome represent only 1 percent of total mineral export earnings.[18] Thus, exports of these commodities could be turned off or manipulated without severely disrupting the flow of foreign exchange to South Africa if the export sale of all other mineral commodities (especially gold) continued. But this very discussion involves the frequent assumption of many in the West that commercial advantage, or "profit" in the Western sense, is always the motive among the socialist nations. This is, of course, faulty thinking.

Cartels inspired or created by Moscow in commodities like chromium would not have to have a Western kind of profit motive. For example, the Soviet Union and its clients could take a temporary loss by dumping (or withholding) commodities produced by the cartel, and look forward to an eventual profit in the form of financial chaos, increased unemployment, and disrupted industrial production in West Europe and in industrialized nations elsewhere.[19]

It is also clear that even if the Soviet Union had no intention of manipulating the supply/prices of minerals produced in Southern Africa, the increasing number of radical governments in the region could mean a decreasing capability to meet fully all minerals delivery requirements. Part of the problem is that political turmoil in Southern Africa could involve sabotage, terrorism, attacks on mining and transportation facilities, labor strikes, civic disorders, and the like. Even having a Marxist regime in power does not guarantee tranquility, as the active anti-government guerrilla movements in Angola, Mozambique, and Ethiopia attest.

It should be noted that even if the Republic of South Africa's nonfuel minerals production and reserves do not come under Soviet direct or indirect manipulation any time soon, there are still numerous ways in which the flow of strategic resources out of and through the waters near South Africa might in the future be disrupted, or perhaps denied, to the West. Possible disruption scenarios include the slow economic strangulation of South Africa to bring pressure on the white minority government; sabotage and terrorism, e.g., by the Soviet-backed Marxist guerrillas in the African National Congress; and, less likely, major military action, perhaps involving Cuban troops and/or Soviet naval forces.[20]

The Soviet Union has an extensive centralized control apparatus dealing with minerals production and supply. Producing as it does nearly all the minerals consumed in a modern industrial economy, the Soviet Union's state monopoly organizations, closely linked to similar organizations in all CMEA countries, provide a means of dealing with, and serving as models for, minerals production operations. The Soviet Union's extensive mineral resources and their central control through state ministries also give the USSR significant advantages that can be used to support Soviet global strategy. Supplies of energy and nonfuel minerals help the Soviet Union to maintain control over East Europe, Mongolia, Vietnam, and Cuba. The following examples suggest that the Soviet Union might indeed take advantage of a substantial degree of control, direct or indirect, over nonfuel minerals in Southern Africa:[21]

o   After the Sino-Soviet break, Moscow severed deliveries of <u>cobalt</u>, <u>chromium</u>, <u>nickel</u>, and <u>oil</u> to the People's Republic of China in hopes of harming China's industrialization efforts.

o   In the 1950s, the USSR and the CMEA exploited Western shortages and exported such commodities as <u>chromium</u>, <u>asbestos</u>, <u>coal</u>, and <u>timber</u> only in exchange for strategic goods and equipment essential for Soviet bloc industrial development.

o   In the late-1950s, the USSR dumped <u>tin</u> on world markets, causing collapse of the price.

o   Through the 1960s, the USSR exported <u>oil</u> and <u>titanium</u> at 40 to 20 percent below market prices.

o   The Soviet Union withdrew <u>platinum</u> from world markets in the 1970s, causing a sharp rise in price to record heights.

o   In the fall of 1979, the USSR suddenly stopped exporting <u>titanium</u> sponge, thus causing a price shock and supply disruptions.

o   In 1982, the USSR dumped <u>nickel</u> in the world market, hurting especially Canadian producers.

Concluding Comments

The Soviet Union certainly has a great many problems at home, especially in the economic arena, but these problems do not seem to be putting substantial restrictions on Soviet efforts to weaken the industrialized nations of the world, including those in West Europe. Moscow's gradual but persistent efforts to diminish the influence of the United States in critically important geopolitical regions of the world and build up its own power are focused intensively on the Persian Gulf and Southern Africa. It is evident that one of the main goals of the USSR is creating a capability for denying or disrupting imports of oil and nonfuel minerals so vitally needed by the economies of the industrialized democracies. This threat of indirect encirclement and control of critical raw materials relied upon by the industrialized democracies is probably more dangerous than the threat of military attack.

At some future date, the economies of West Europe, the United States, and East Asia could be at the mercy of newly established Marxist-Leninist governments dominated by Moscow. In that event, tremendous international leverage could be brought to bear by far-sighted Soviet strategic planners bent on inducing democratic societies to accommodate Soviet political objectives.

NOTES

1. For more in-depth treatment of the author's view that the United States, its allies in West Europe, and Japan are increasingly vulnerable to cutoffs or at least to sharp price escalations in imports of energy and nonfuel minerals, see: James Arnold Miller, A White Paper -- "The Resource War" and the U.S. Business Community: A Case for a Council on Economics and National Security (New York: National Strategy Information Center, 1980): James Arnold Miller, Struggle for Survival: Strategic Minerals and the West (Washington, D.C.: American African Affairs Association, 1980); and, James Arnold Miller, "The Resource War and the Need for a Comprehensive and Coherent U.S. Minerals and Materials Policy," paper presented at the 1982 Summer National Meeting of the American Institute of Chemical Engineers, Cleveland, Ohio, August 31, 1982.

2. Leonid Brezhnev, cited in Robert Moss, "Reaching for Oil: The Soviets' Bold Mideast Strategy," Saturday Review, April 12, 1980, p. 22.

3. These themes were drawn to a large degree from the excellent paper by Frank R. Barnett, "Reclaiming the Initiative from the Soviet Heartland: The Case for a Tri-Oceanic Alliance of the Imperiled Rimlands" (New York: National Strategy Information Center, 1980).

4. See Bohdan O. Szuprowicz, How to Avoid Strategic Materials Shortages: Dealing with Cartels, Embargoes, and Supply Disruptions (New York: John Wiley and Sons, 1981), p. 43-80, and passim.

5. Roberta Hornig, "Brown Cites Soviet Oil Cutoff Fear," Washington Star, May 4, 1977, p. A-1; "CIA Chief Foresees 'Vicious Struggle' as Oil Output Falls," Washington Post, April 23, 1980, p. A-32; and, "Soviet Competition for Mideast Oil Predicted," Washington Star, April 22, 1980, p. A-8.

6. Szuprowicz, pp. 79-80.

7. James McCartney, "Preparing to Protect the West's Oil Supplies," Journal of Commerce, March 9, 1984, p. 4.

8. See Jan S. Breemer, "The Tanker War: Not Quite A Full-Blown Crisis," Seapower, April 15, 1985, pp. 50-56. This outstanding article provides extensive details and a chart listing all 40 ships attacked in the Persian Gulf from March 1 to December 3, 1984, to include the dates, tonnage, and flag of each vessel, and identity of the attacker (Iraq or Iran).

9. Stansfield Turner, "Terrorism's New Weapon: Mines at Sea," Christian Science Monitor, August 27, 1984, p. 14.

10. James McCartney, "Preparing to Protect the West's Oil Supplies," Journal of Commerce, March 9, 1984, p. 4.

11. "U.S. Vulnerability to Oil Cutoff Seen," New York Times,

September 18, 1983, p. A-11.

12. An article dealing with the possibilities for maritime terrorism is Christopher C. Joyner, "Offshore Maritime Terrorism: International Implications and the Legal Response," Naval War College Review, July-August 1983, pp. 17-31.

13. See Robert Moss, "Reaching for Oil: The Soviets' Bold Mideast Strategy," Saturday Review, April 12, 1980, p. 22; and, Walter S. Mossberg, "As Mideast Heats Up, U.S. Frets Over Peril to the Saudi Oil Fields," Wall Street Journal, January 21, 1980, p. 1.

14. James Arnold Miller, Struggle for Survival, passim; and, James Arnold Miller, Daniel I. Fine, and R. Daniel McMichael, eds., The Resource War in 3-D: Dependency, Diplomacy, Defense (Pittsburgh: World Affairs Council of Pittsburgh, 1980).

15. See James Arnold Miller, "Hard Choices: The Continuing U.S. Minerals Dependency, and What's Being Done About It," Sea Power, April 1984, pp. 100-110. It should be noted that because of unsatisfactory provisions governing the regulation of deep seabed mining, the United Nations' Law of the Sea Treaty was rejected by President Reagan in 1982.

16. See U.S. Bureau of Mines, Mineral Commodity Summaries - 1985, as well as the monthly "Mineral Industry Summaries" published by the U.S. Bureau of Mines, on the respective nonfuel commodities.

17. U.S. Bureau of Mines, Mineral Commodity Summaries - 1985, "Cobalt," pp. 36-37.

18. South African Minerals Bureau, "U.S. Minerals Policy 1979: Assessment of the Importance of Nonfuel Mineral Supplies from South Africa" (Pretoria, Republic of South Africa: South African Minerals Bureau, Briefing Paper no. 10, 1981).

19. This point has been made by Frank R. Barnett, "Reclaiming the Initiative from the Soviet Heartland: The Case for a Tri-Oceanic Alliance of the Imperiled Rimlands" (New York: National Strategy Information Center, 1980).

20. Concerning such scenarios, see the discussion in W.C.J. van Rensburg, "A Strategic Mineral Policy for the Free World," paper presented at the Second World Balance of Power Conference, Leeds Castle, Kent, England, July 1982. See also "South Africa: The Case Against Disinvestment and Economic Sanctions," ALARM, no. 98, December 1984, pp. 1-8; "South Africa: Political Reform Attempts and Violence," ALARM, no. 97, December 1984, pp. 1-10; and, "Namibia and Angola," ALARM, no. 96, November 1984, pp. 1-4.

21. Szuprowicz, passim.

CONTRIBUTORS

Yonah Alexander. Professor and Director, Institute for Studies in International Terrorism, State University of New York; Senior Fellow, United States Global Strategy Council, Washington, D.C.

Ray S. Cline. Chairman, United States Global Strategy Council, Washington, D.C.; Professor of International Relations, Georgetown University, Washington, D.C.; Former Director, Bureau of Intelligence and Research, U.S. Department of State; Former Deputy Director for Intelligence, Central Intelligence Agency.

Roger E. Kanet. Professor and Head, Political Science Department, University of Illinois at Urbana-Champaign; Sovietologist specializing in Soviet foreign policy.

Daniel R. Kempton. Graduate student in the Department of Political Science at the University of Illinois at Urbana-Champaign.

Jonathan V. Luxmoore. Researcher, Institute for European Defence and Strategy Studies, London, England; specialist in European defense issues.

James Arnold Miller. Executive Director, United States Global Strategy Council, Washington, D.C.; Chairman, Interaction Systems Incorporated, Vienna, Virginia; Editor, <u>Alert Letter on the Availability of Raw Materials</u>; former counterintelligence officer, U.S. Air Force.

Phillip A. Petersen. Assistant for Europe, Office of Policy Support Programs, Office of the Secretary of Defense; previously Intelligence Research Analyst, Defense Intelligence Agency, specializing in Soviet and Warsaw Pact matters.

Giuseppe Schiavone. Professor, University of Catania, Italy; specialist on international organization, East-West trade.

Wolfgang Seiffert. Professor, Faculty of Law, Christian-Albrechts-University, Kiel, Federal Republic of Germany; specialist in international law.

Finn Sollie. Director, Fridtjof Nansen Institute, Lysaker, Norway; Deputy Chairman, Norwegian Institute of International Affairs; specialist in Scandinavian security matters.

Gerhard Wettig. Staff Member, Federal Institute for Eastern and International Studies, Köln, Federal Republic of Germany; specialist on Soviet and Warsaw Pact foreign policies and East-West relations.

INDEX

Abu Nidal Faction, 83
Adomeit, Hannes, 100
Afghanistan, 12, 18-19, 20, 21, 44, 97, 106, 108, 148
AFNORTH. See North Atlantic Treaty Organization, North European Command
African National Congress, 150
Agca, Ali, 86
Air defense forces, 25
Air Forces, 11, 25
Alexander II (tsar), 82
Algeria, 62, 110
Allende, Salvador, 100
Allied Forces, 127. See also North Atlantic Treaty Organization
Amin, Hafizullah, 18
Andropov, Yuri, 5, 57, 76-77, 86
Anglia, 75
Angola, 12, 16, 18, 20, 146, 150
Antinuclear movement. See Peace movements
Arab-Israeli conflict, 19, 106, 108
Armenian Secret Army for the Liberation of Armenia (ASALA), 83
Arms control, 48-50, 96
Arms race, 16-17, 101
ASALA. See Armenian Secret Army for

the Liberation of Armenia
Asbestos, 151
Assad, Hafez al-, 19
Augran, Rene, 84
Austria, 134

BAM line, 125
Barnett, Frank R., 146
Basque Nation and Liberty, 83
Beria, L.P., 135
Brandt, Willy, 137
Brezhnev, Leonid, 3, 4, 17, 20, 53 (n11), 55, 56, 57, 67 (n3), 76, 137, 145
Brown, Harold, 147

Capitalist decline, 3, 4, 67 (n1). See also World revolution
Cappuzo, Umberto, 105
Carnot, Sadi, 82
Cartels, 149, 150
Carter, Jimmy, 20, 97
CDE. See Conference on Confidence-Building Measures and Disarmament in Europe
CDU/CSU. See Federal Republic of Germany, "big coalition"
Central Group of Forces (CGF), 25
Central planning, 13
CGF. See Central Group of

160

Stent, Angela, 15, 97–98
Strategic directions, 31–32, 34
Strategic offensive, 35
Strategic Rocket Forces (SRF), 25
Strategic thinking, 7–10
Strategy
   defined, 27
   military doctrine and, 26
   sectors. See Napravleniye
   See also Decoupling strategy; Global strategy; Strategic directions; Strategic offensive, Strategic thinking
Submarines, 127
Supreme High Command (SHC), 33
Suslov, Mikhail, 4, 42
Sweden, 129, 130, 131
Syria, 19, 106, 107, 108, 110

Tactics, 27, 28
Taiwan. See Republic of China
Tank armies, 31
Taraki, Nur Mohammad, 18
Technology, 13–14, 15, 62–63, 65, 68(n17), 97, 124
Terrorism, 17–18, 21
   countermeasures, 87–88
   Soviet support for, 84–88
   state sponsored, 81–82, 87–88
   targets, 83–84
   twentieth-century, 82–84
Thatcher, Margaret, 74, 77
Theaters of military action (TMA), 29–32, 34, 36–37
Theaters of War (T.W.), 28–29
"Theory of the Navy," 27

Third World, 17, 18
   disillusionment in, 21
   resource war and, 146
   Soviet economic presence, 15–16
Timber, 151
Tin, 151
Titanium, 151
TMA. See Theaters of military action
Trade relations, 20, 56–57, 97, 98–99
   with Federal Republic of Germany, 136
   national interests and, 15
   with Soviet bloc, 58–60
   with United States, 14, 15, 56, 97, 98
   with West Europe, 64, 65, 78
Trans-Siberian Railroad, 125
Treaty concerning the Basis for Relations Between the FRG and the GDR, 138, 140
Turkey, 106, 107, 110, 111, 113–114
T.V. See Theaters of war
TVD. See Theaters of military action
T.W. See Theaters of war

Umberto (king of Italy), 82
United Red Army, 83
United States, 1–4, 87–88, 147
   basing privileges, 109, 111–113, 115, 116
   deterrent strategies, 46
   economic sanctions by, 56, 97, 98
   grain sales by, 14
   Greece and, 111–112, 113, 115
   Jackson-Vanik amendment, 56